FASHION CATS UNCHAINED

PLUS

KILLER BUNNIES, ZOMBIE SANTAS & OTHER MAD MALARKEY

COLORING BOOK

FASHION CATS
Unchained
Coloring Book

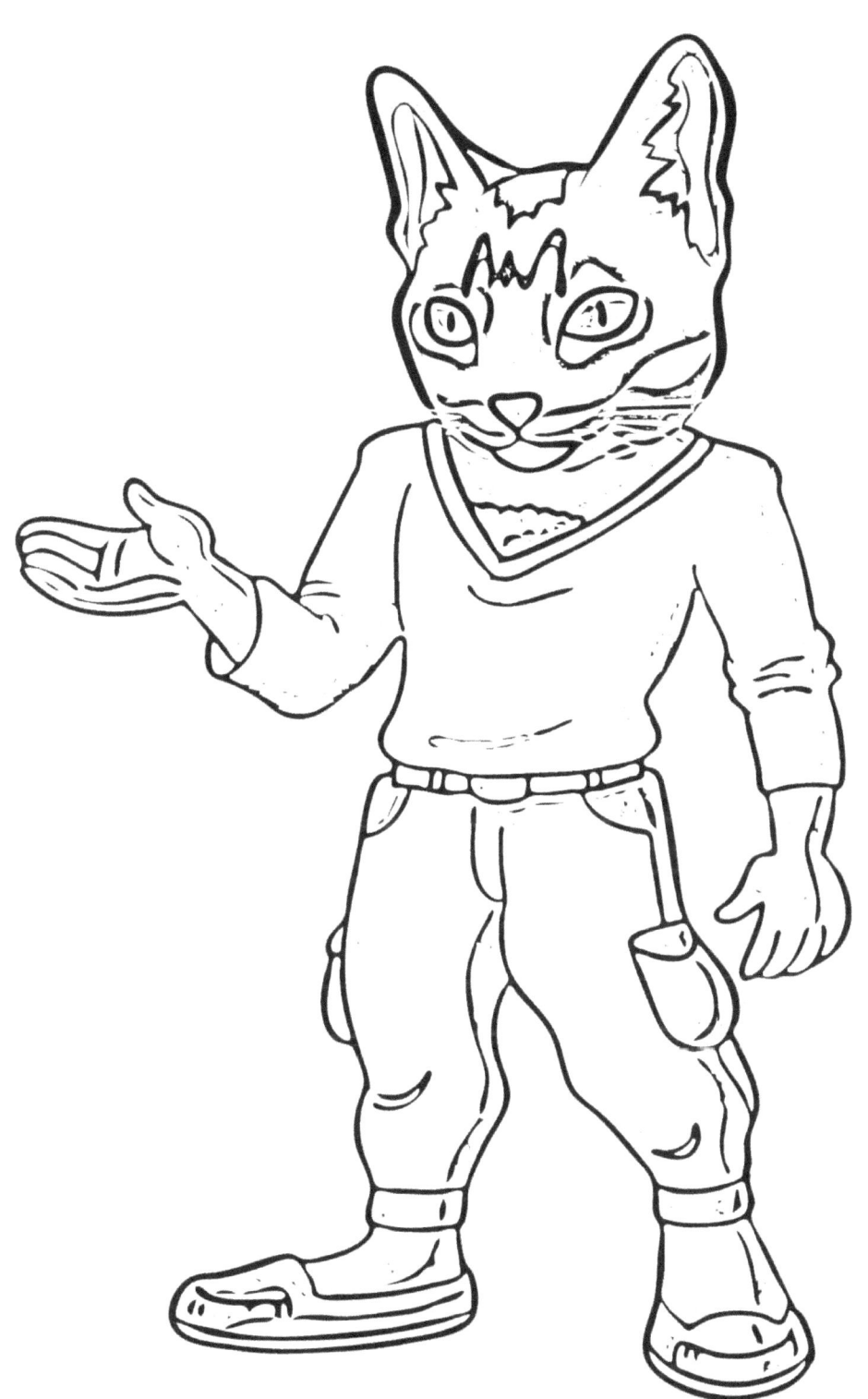

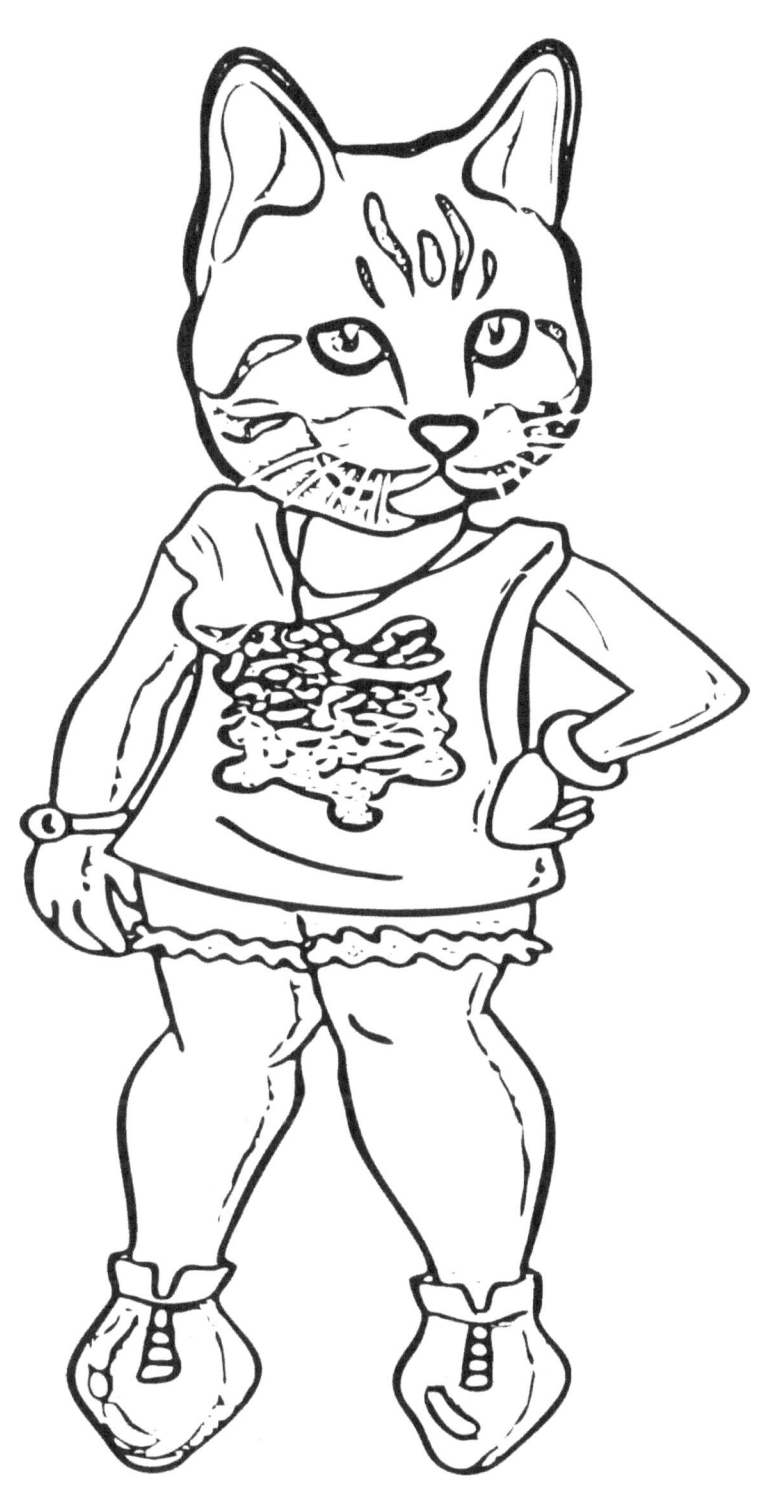

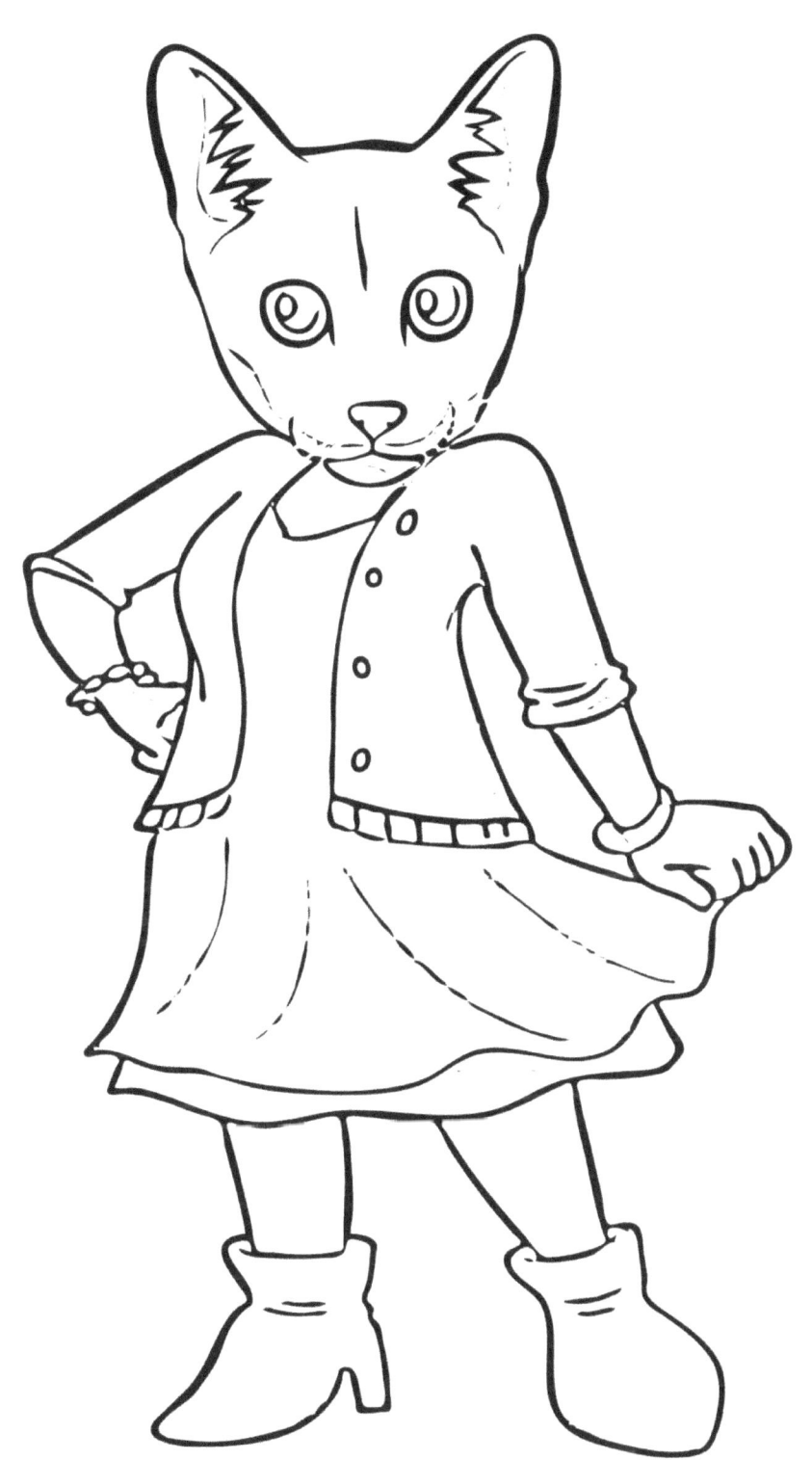

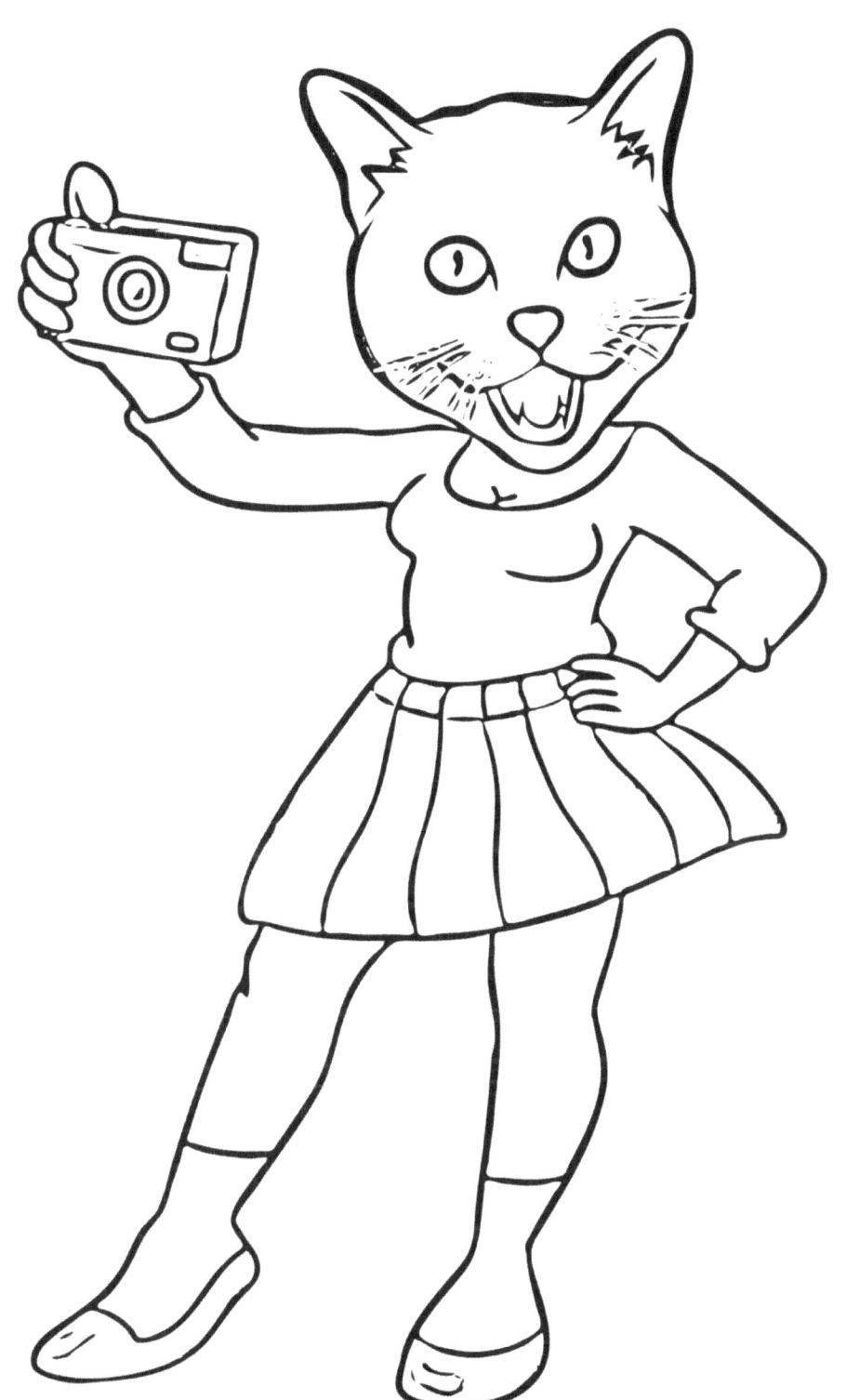

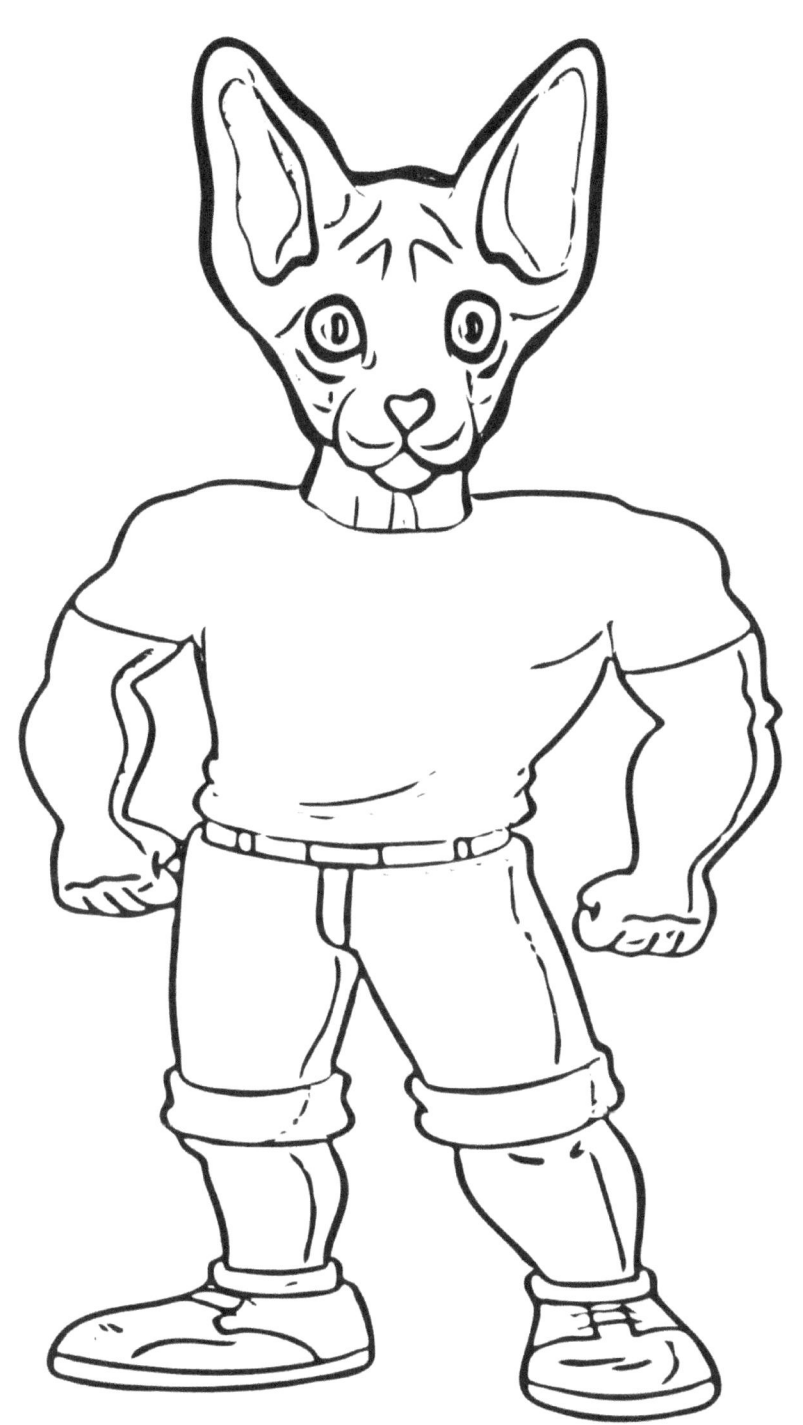

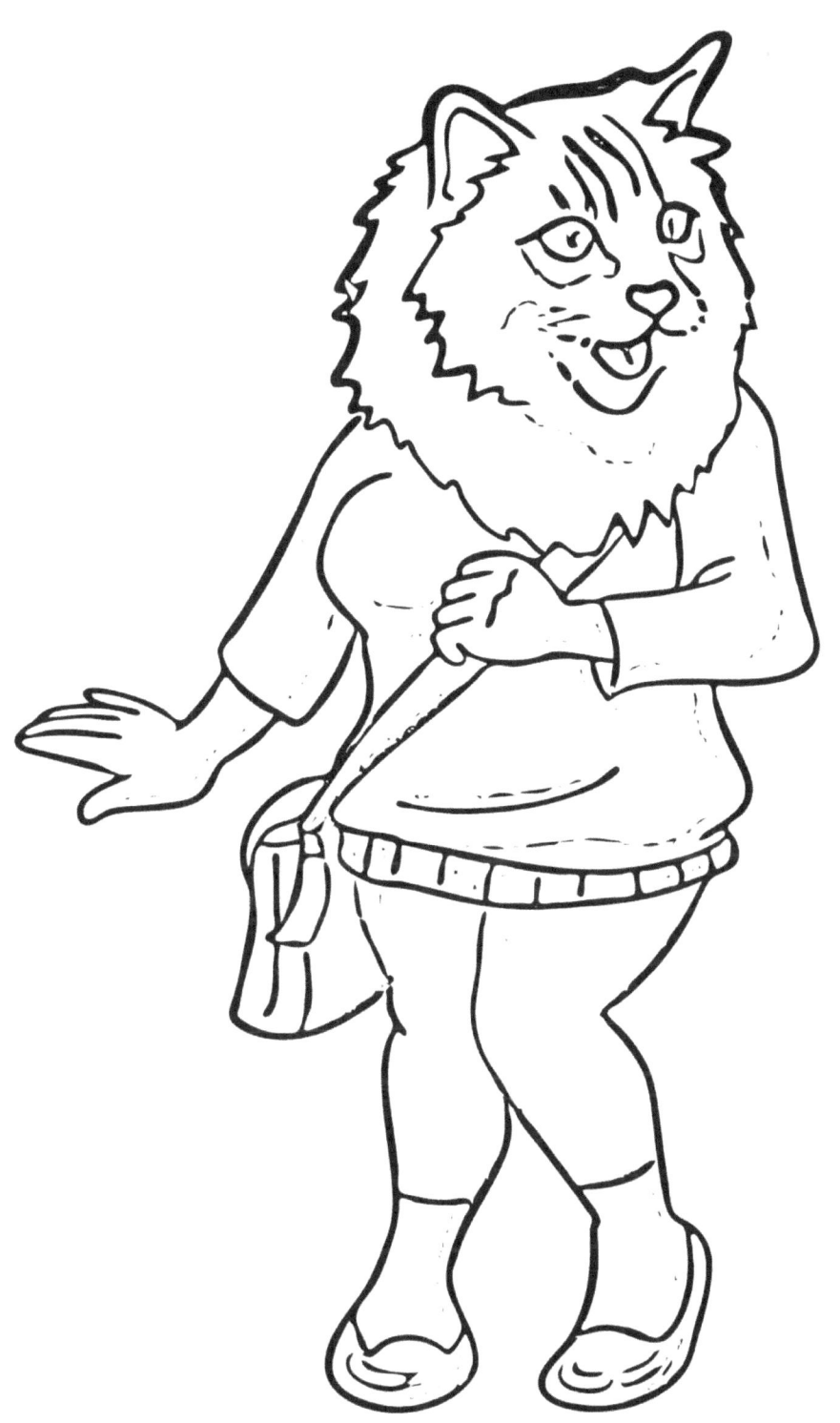

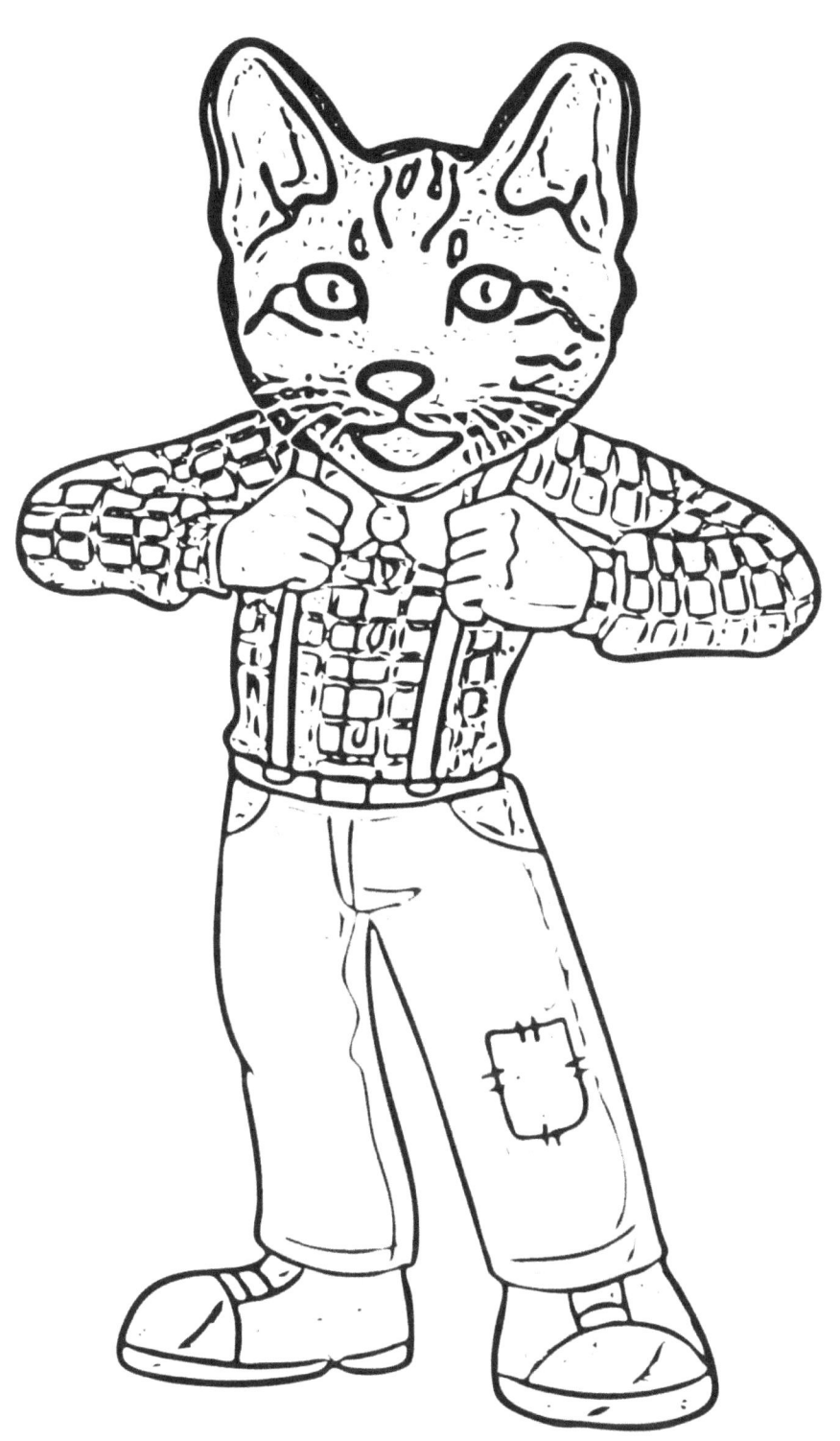

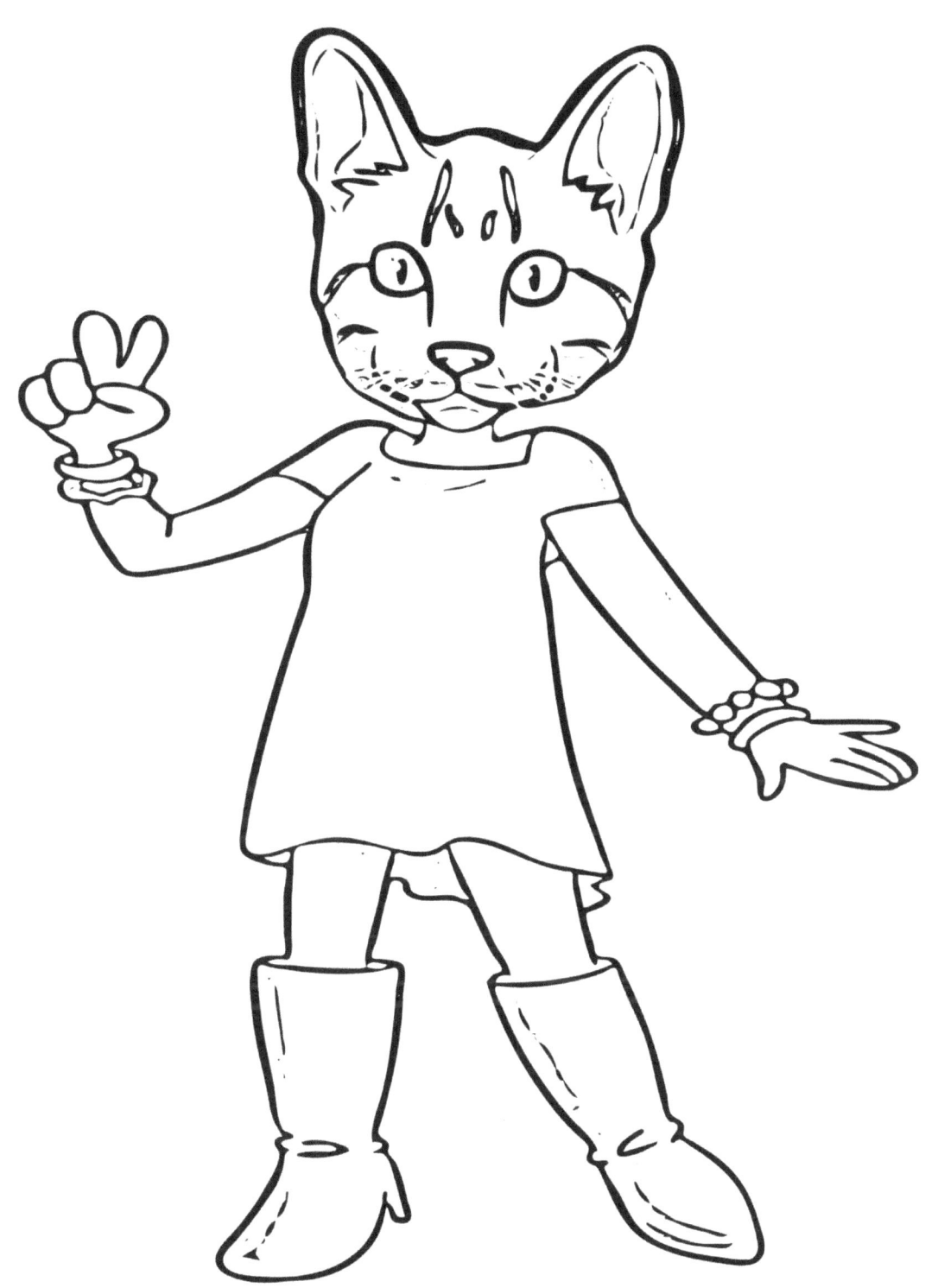

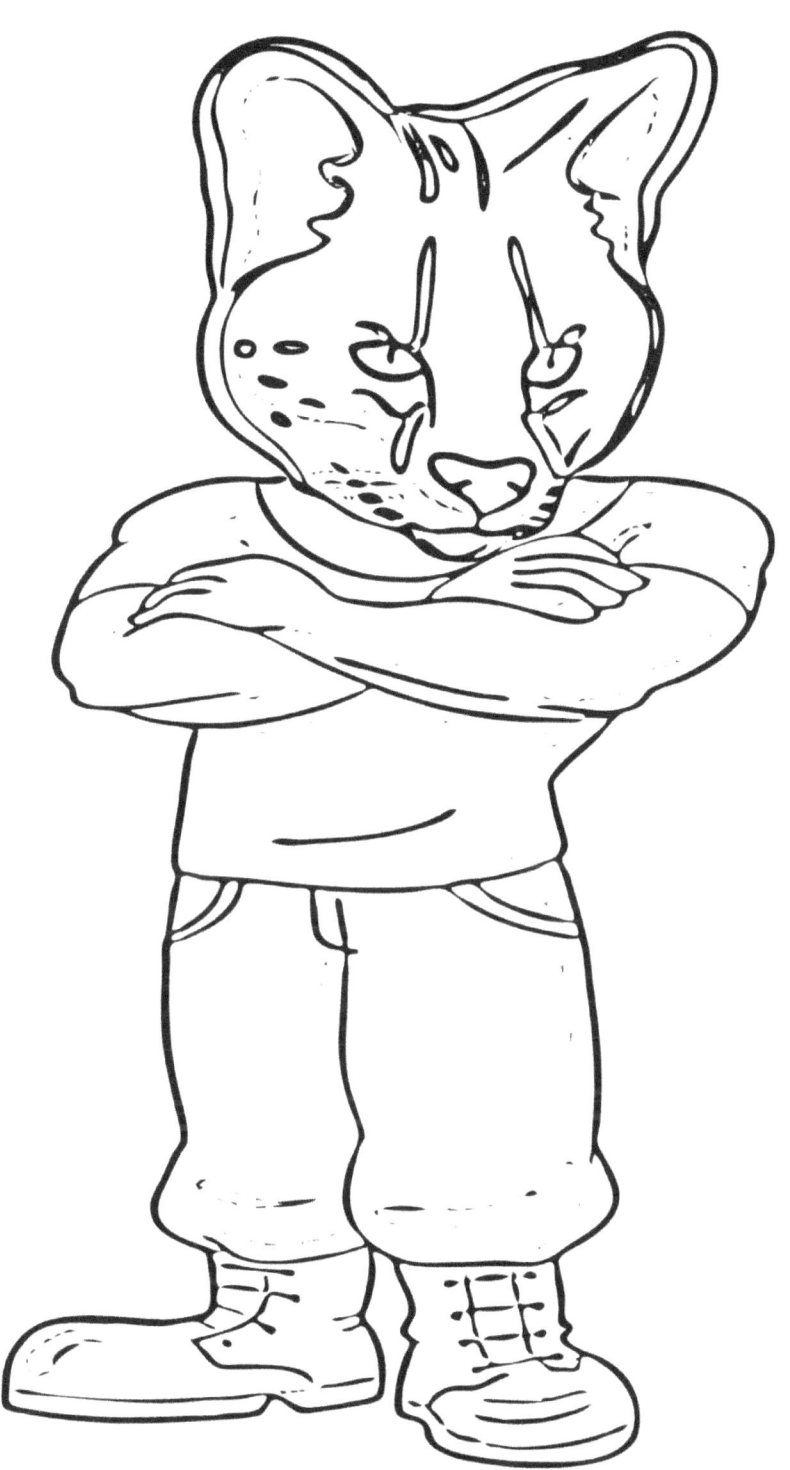

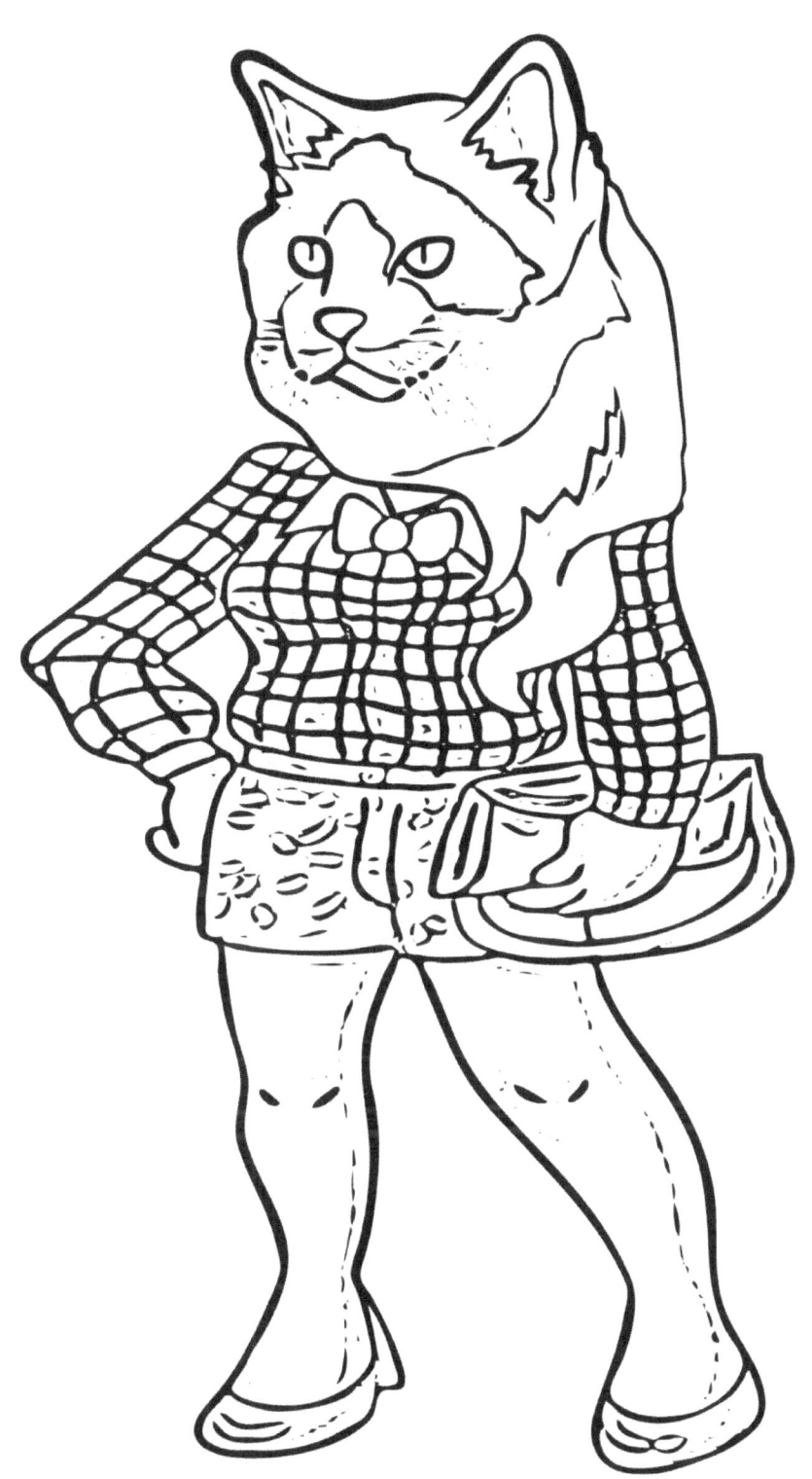

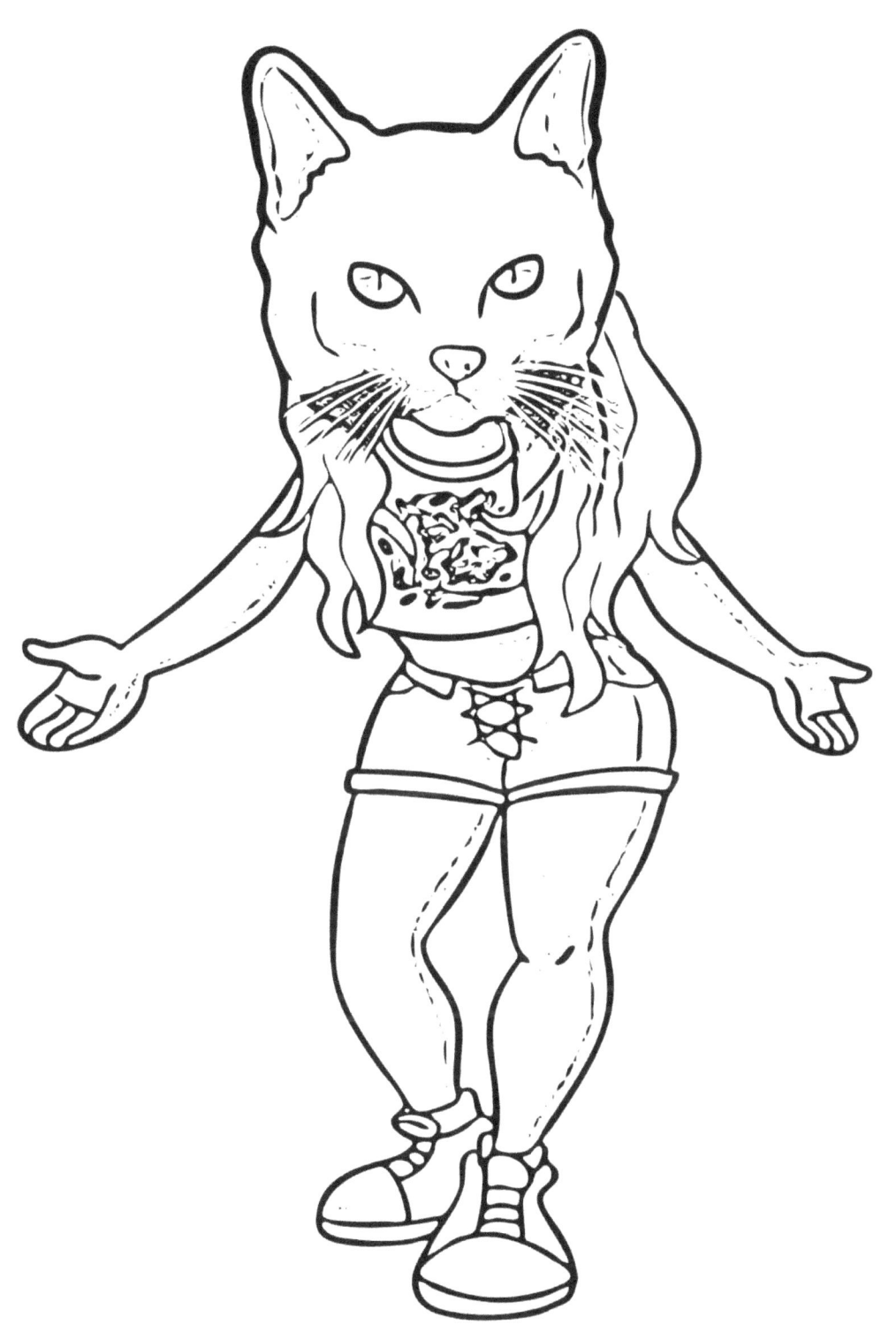

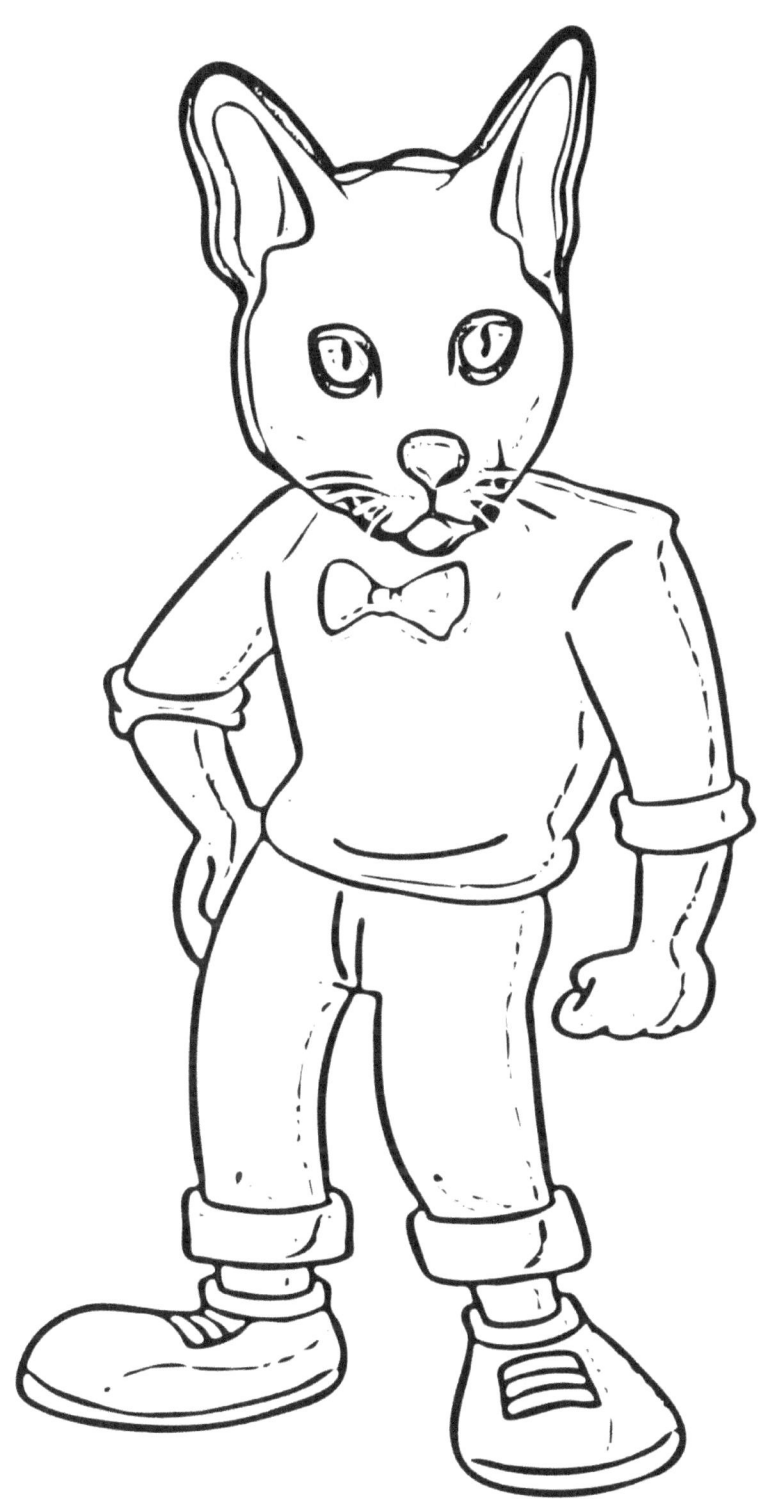

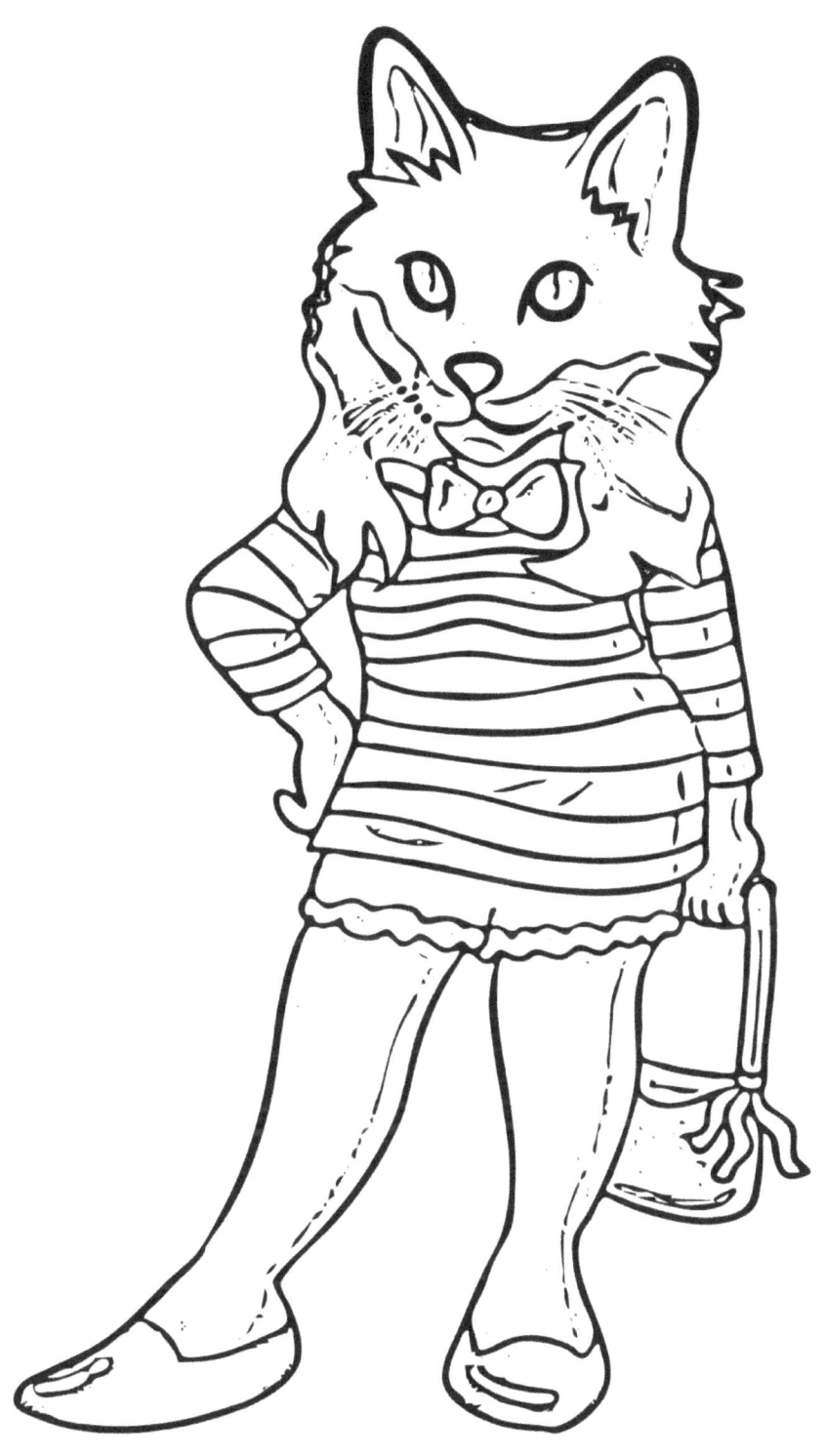

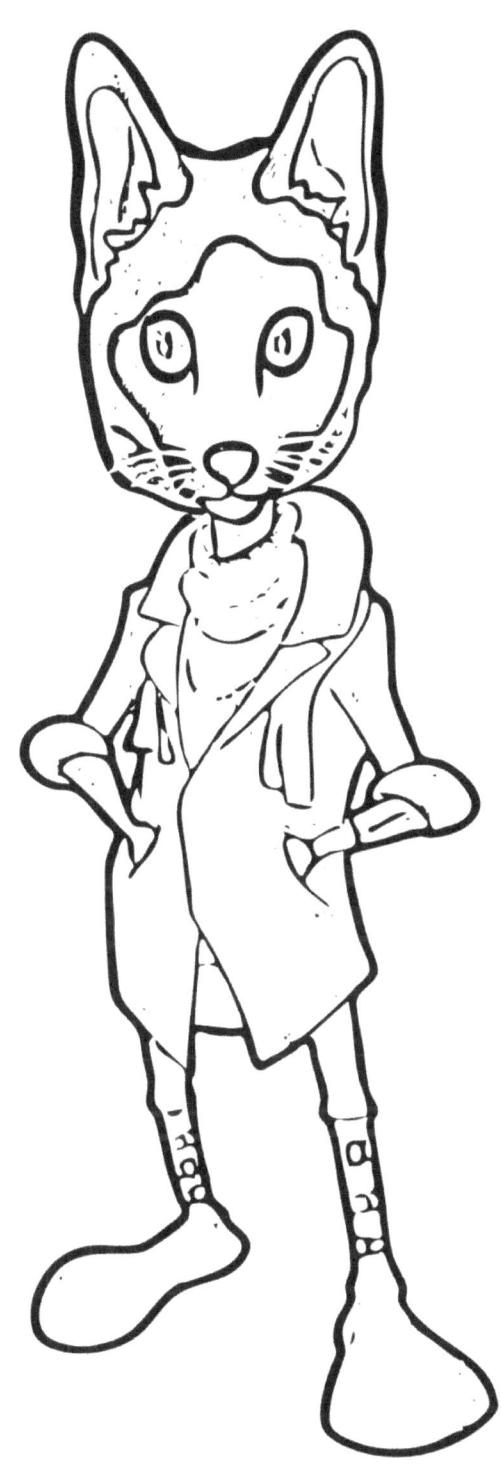

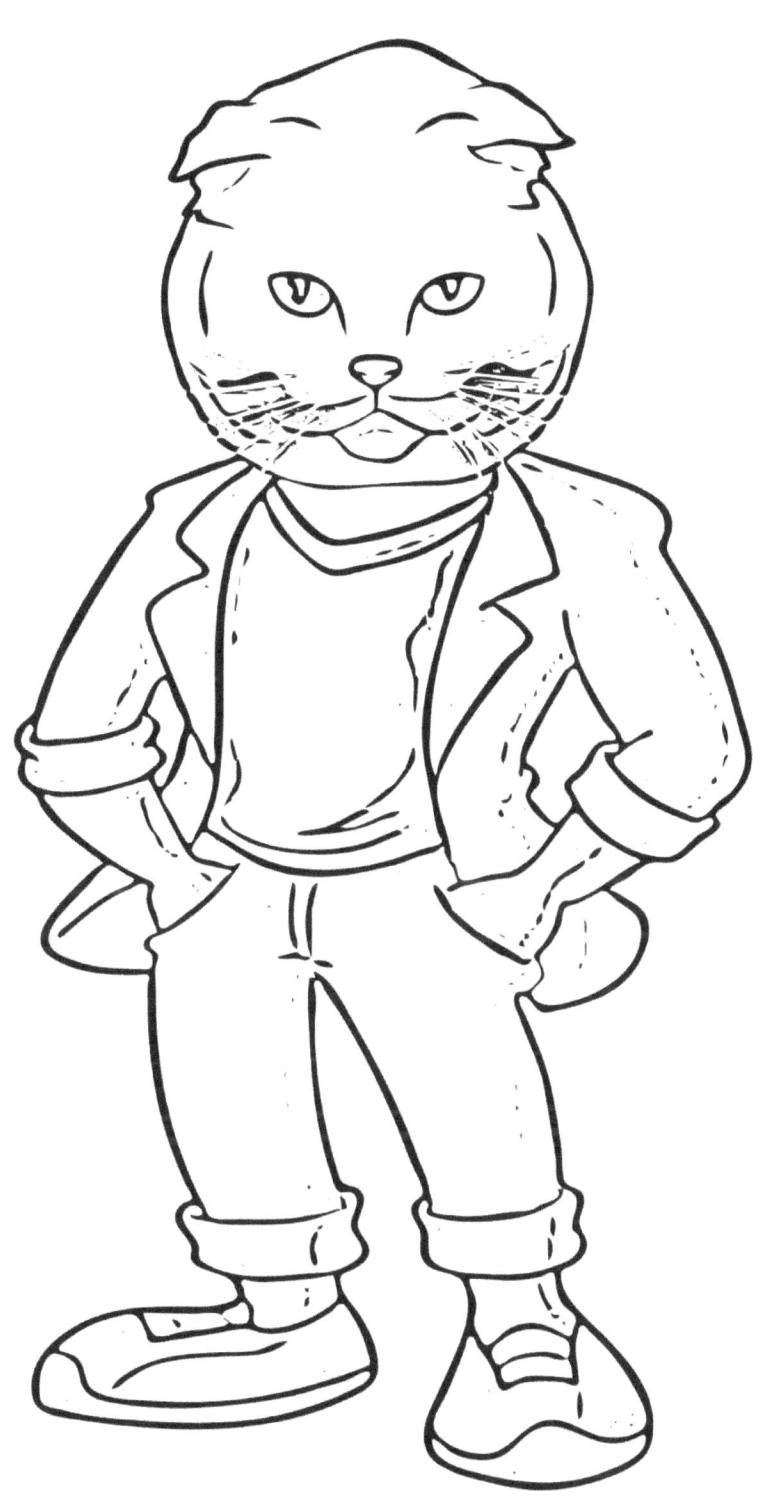

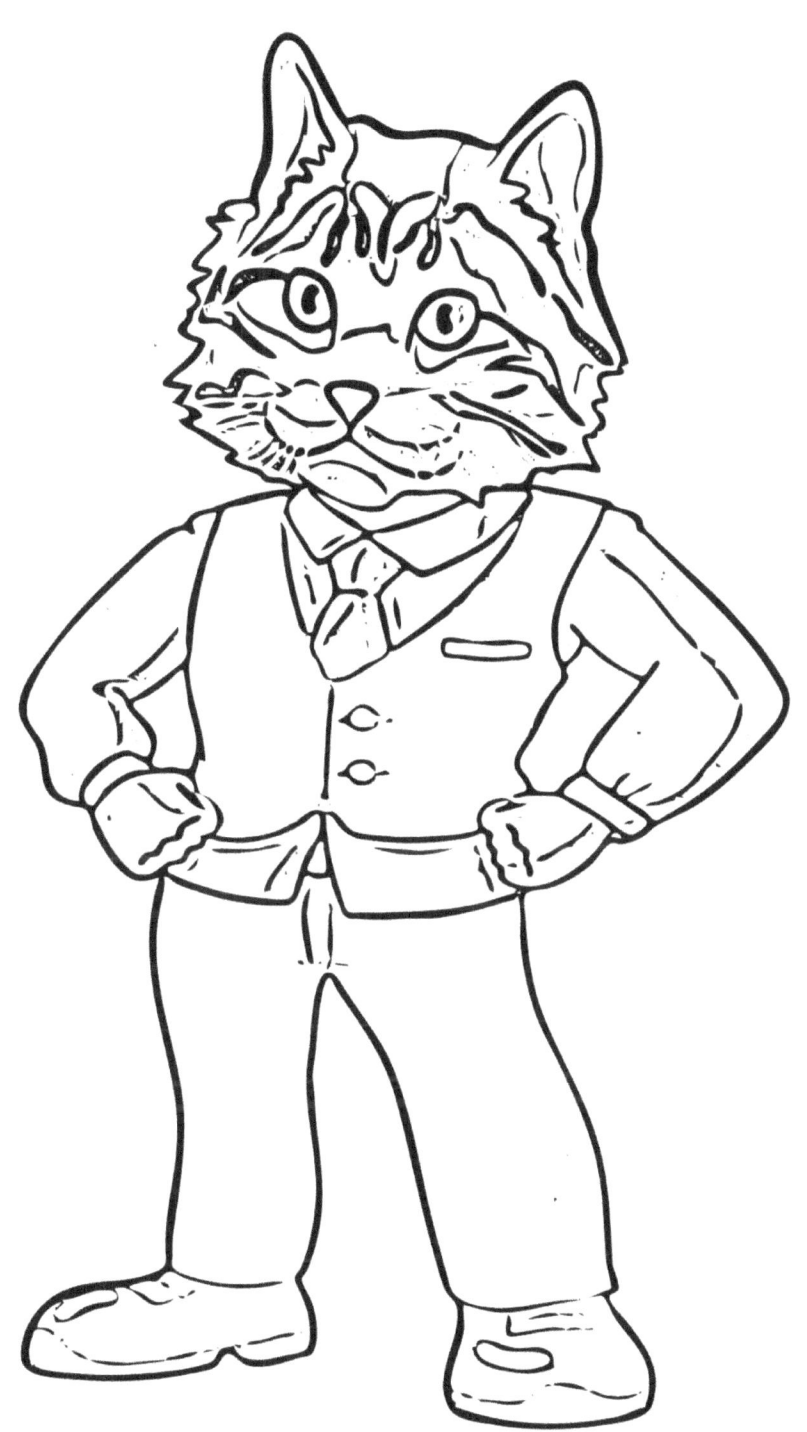

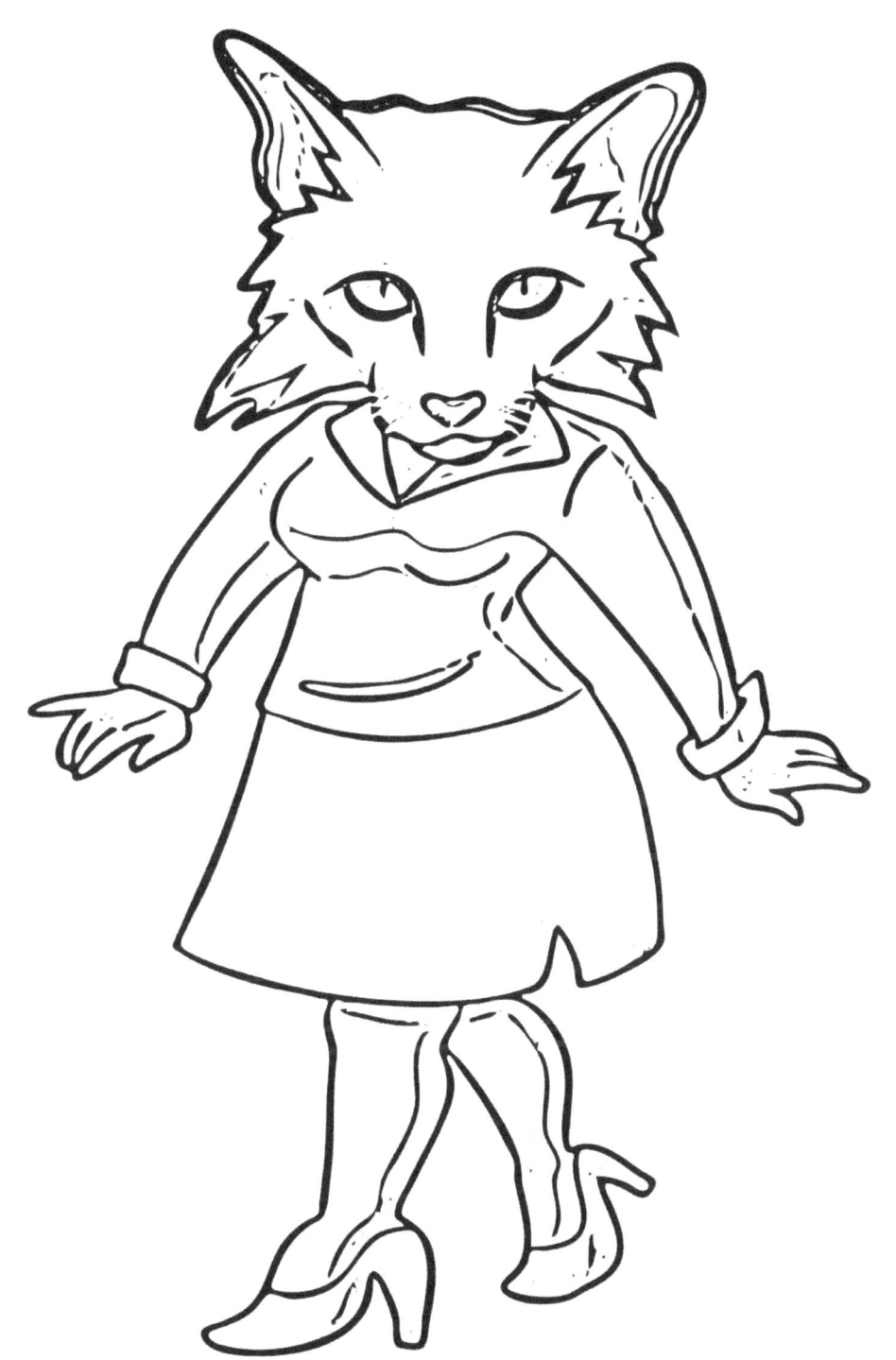

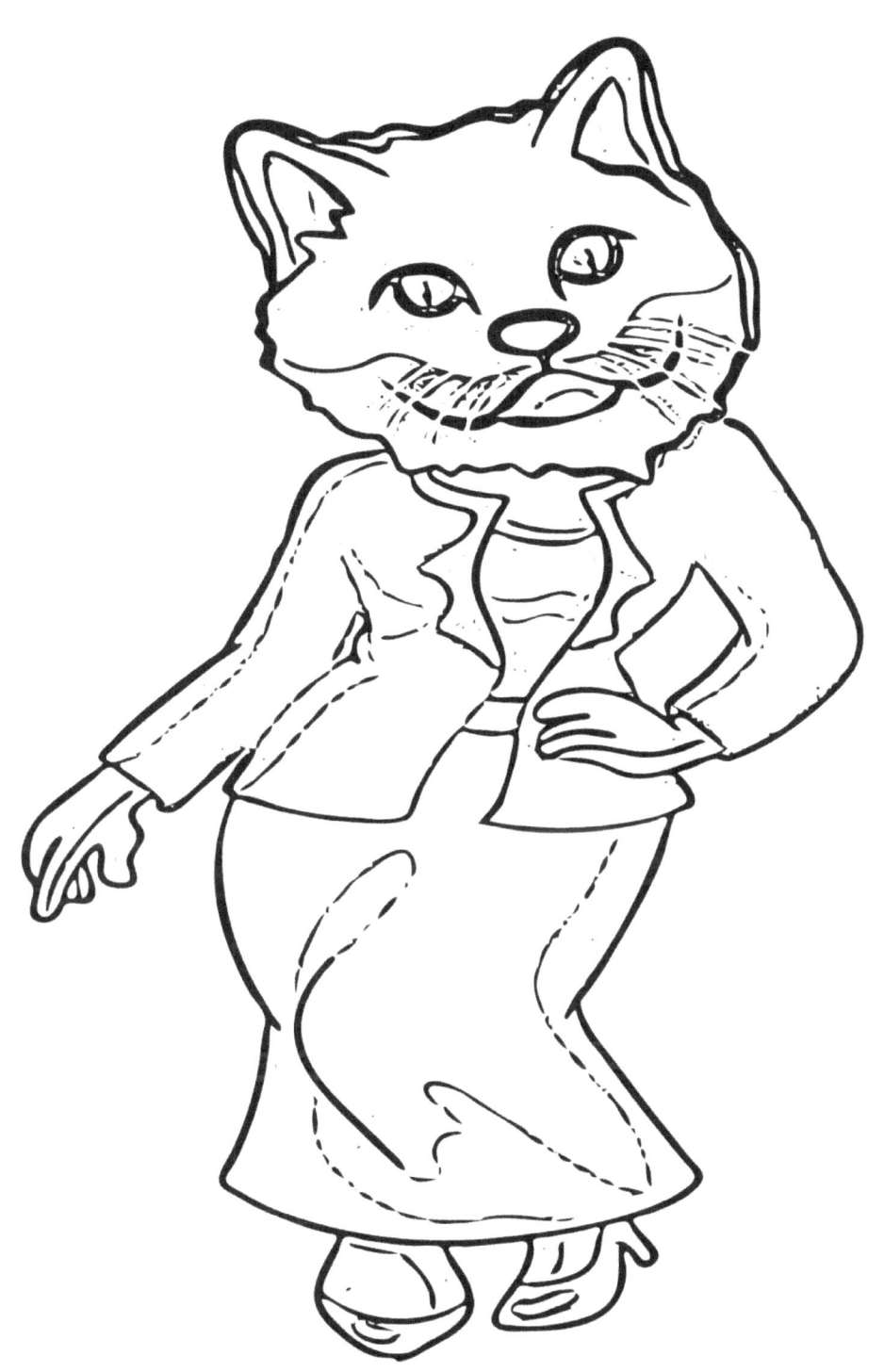

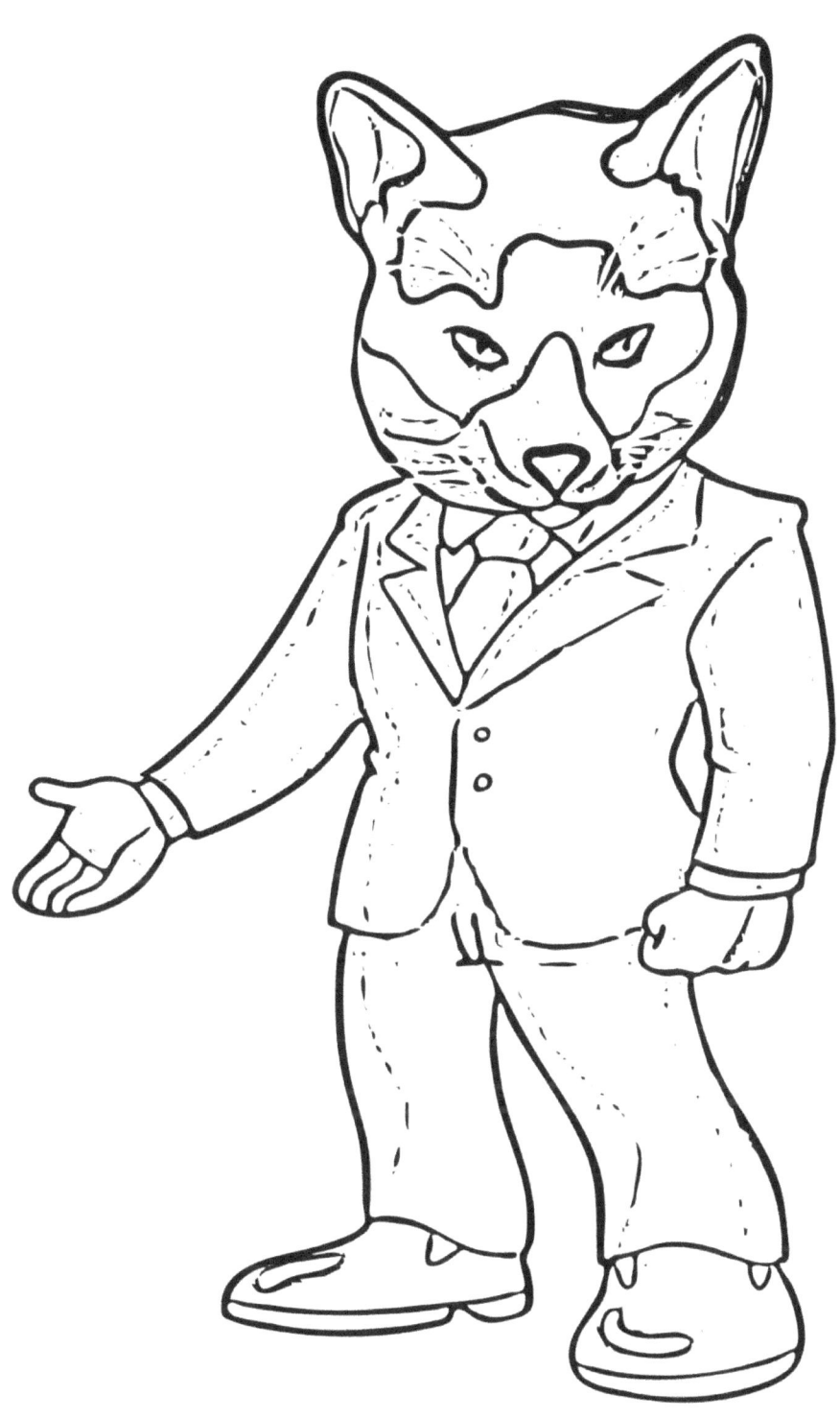

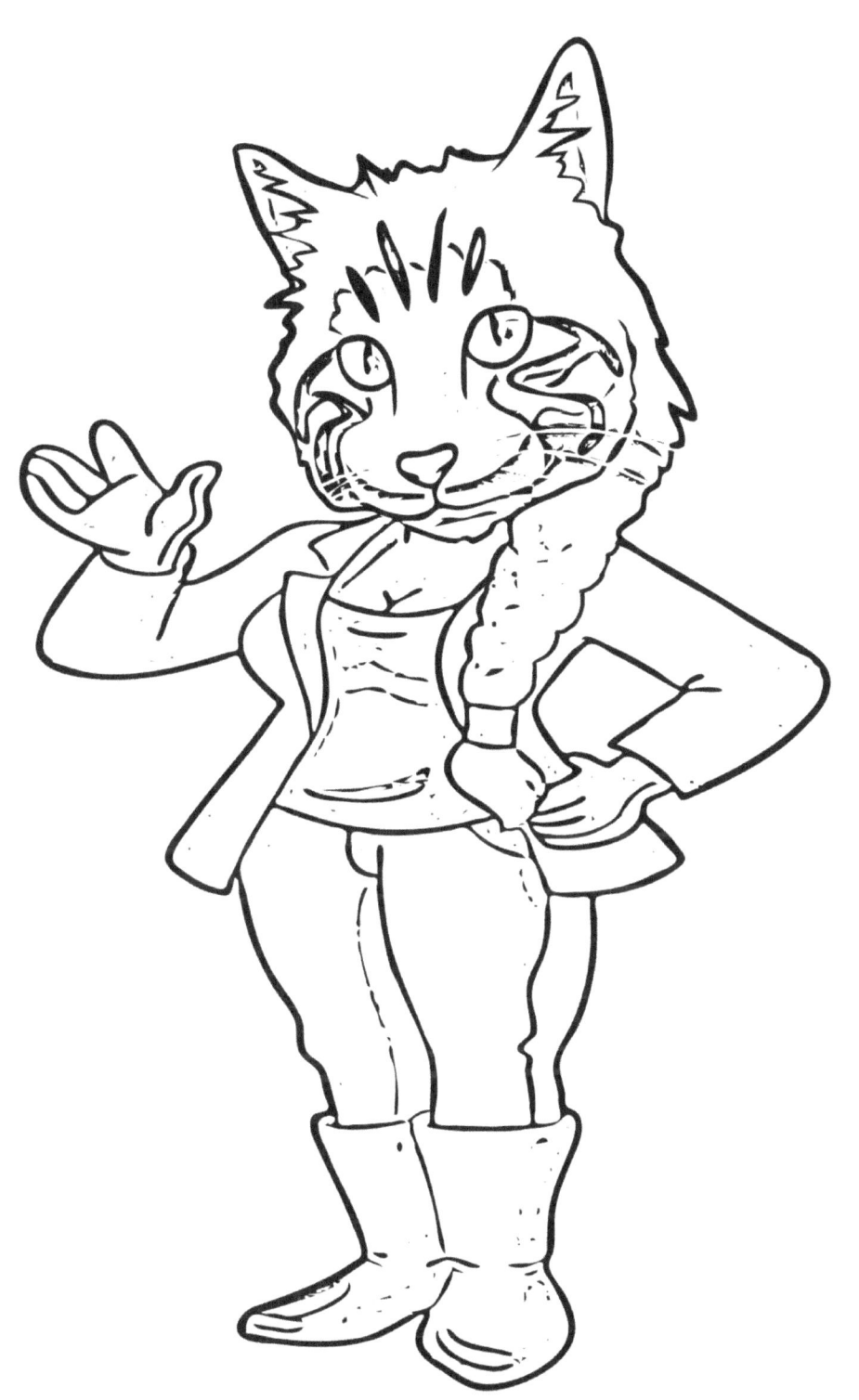

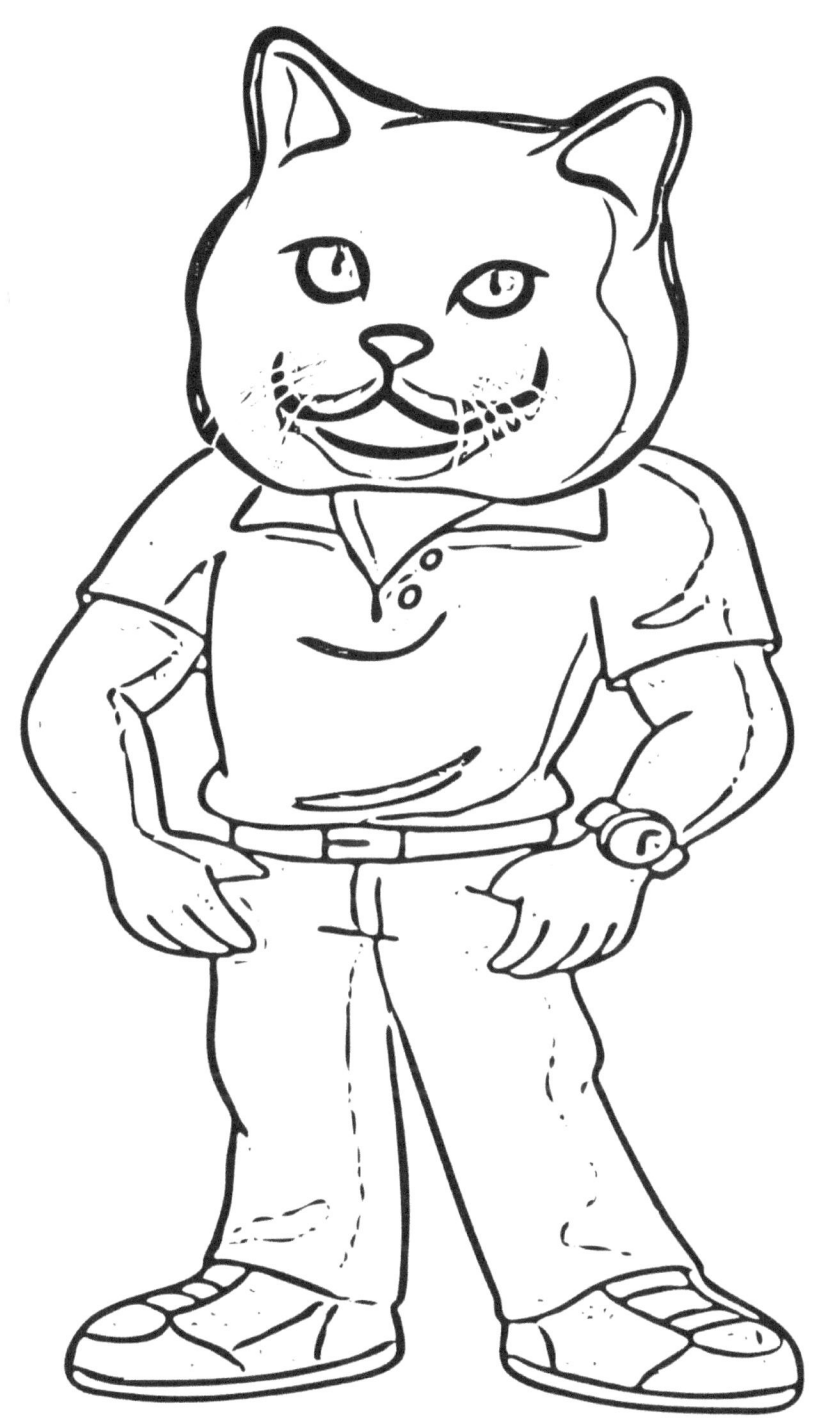

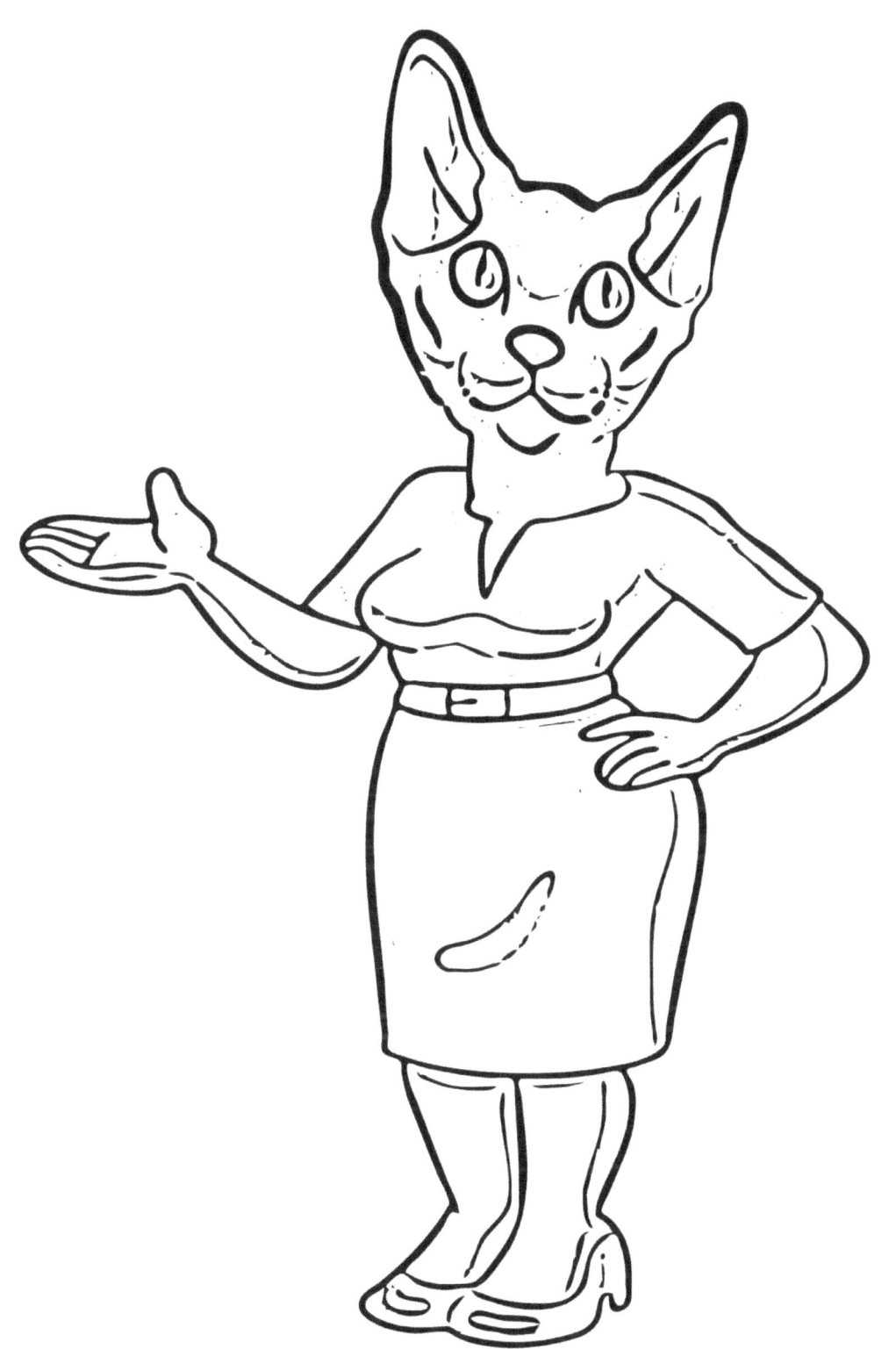

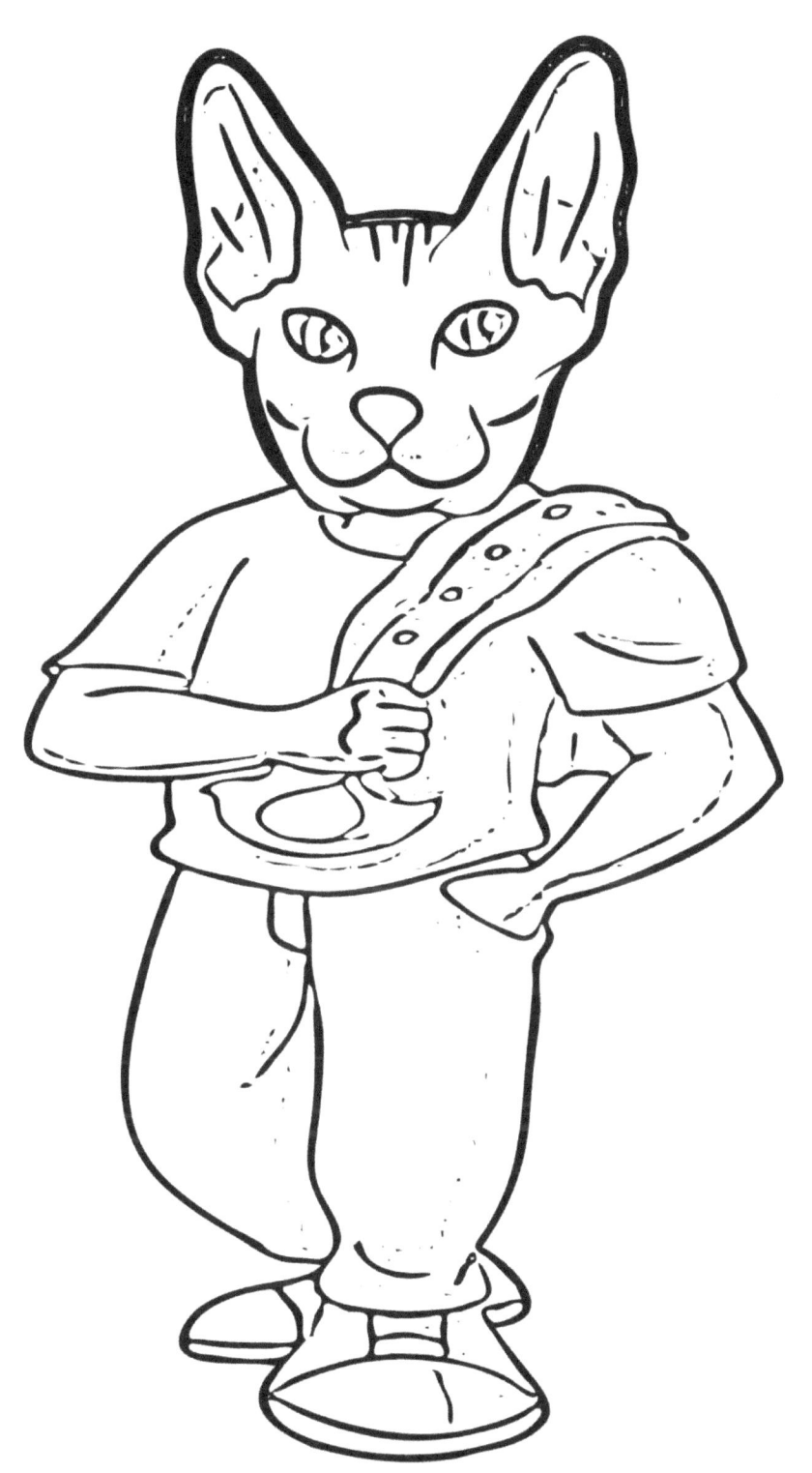

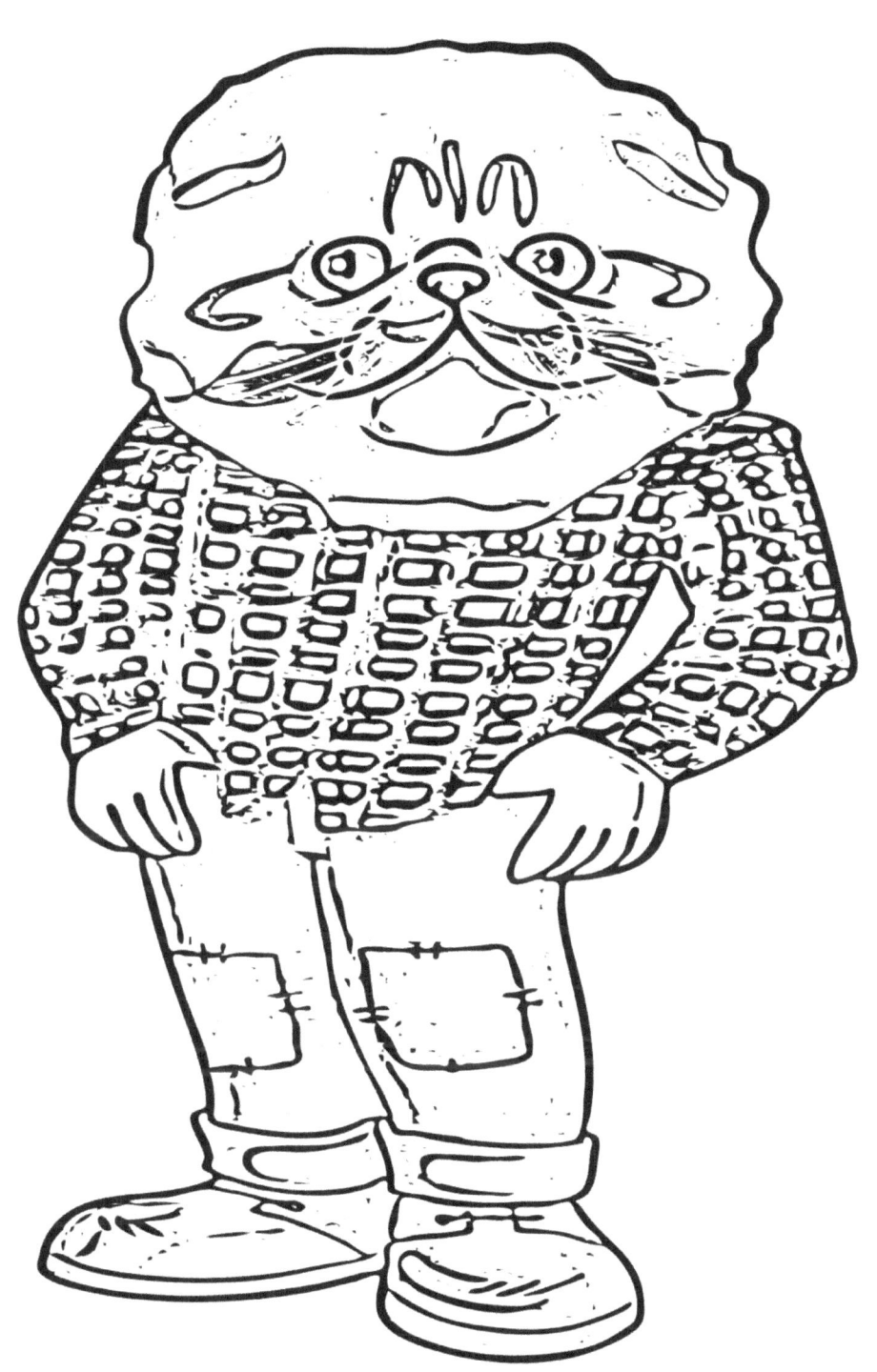

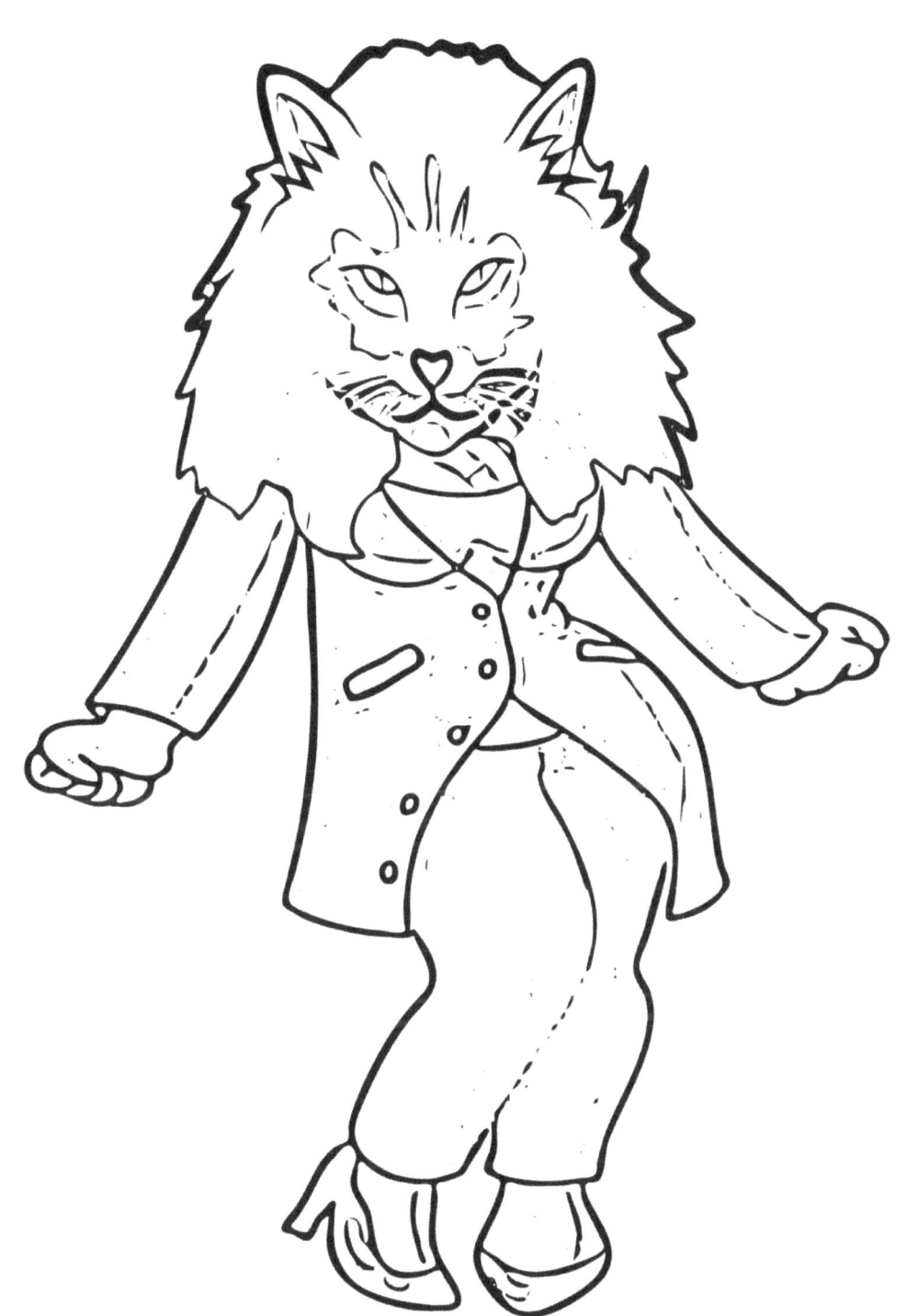

KILLER BUNNIES, ZOMBIE SANTAS & OTHER MAD MALARKEY

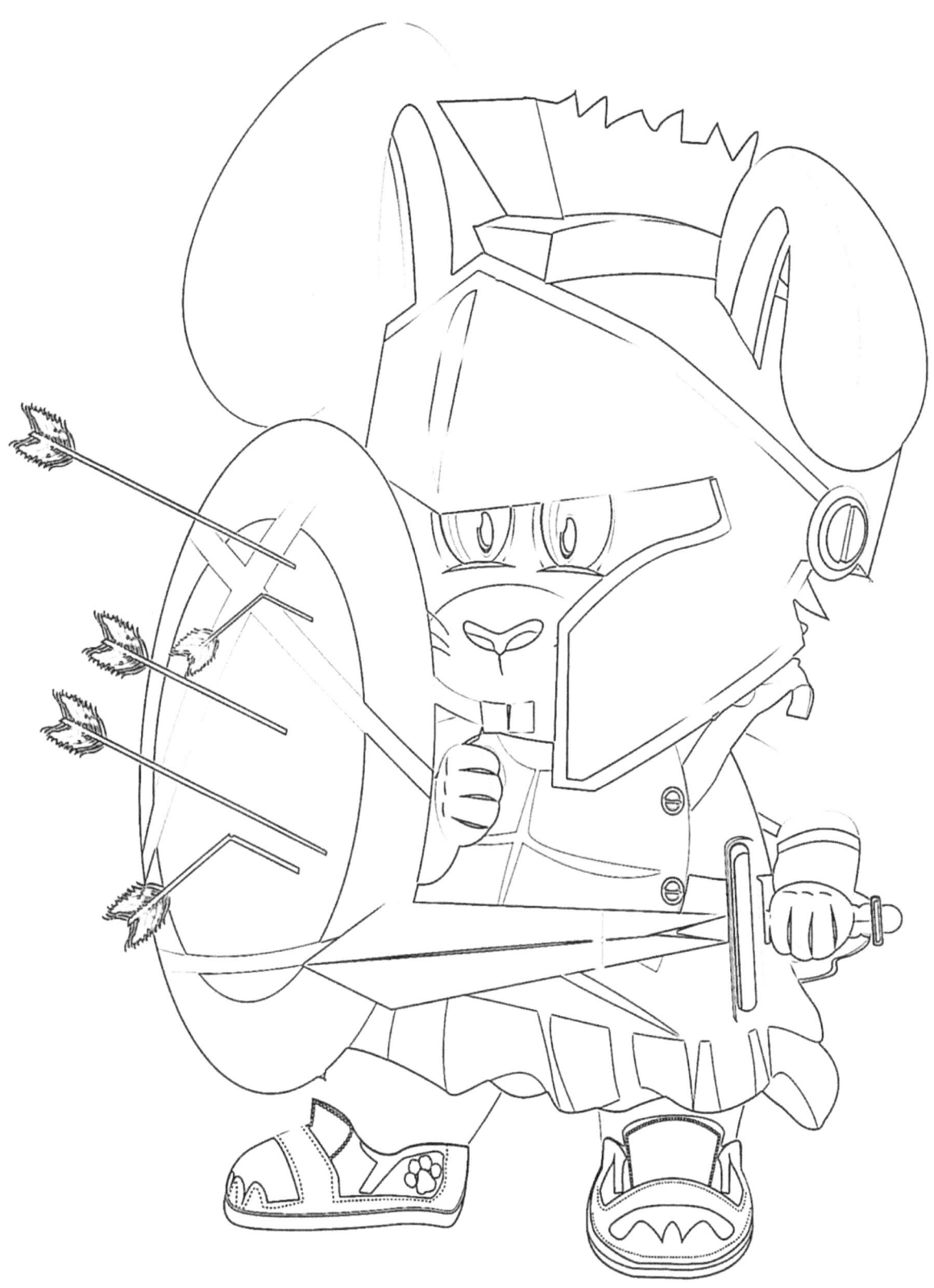

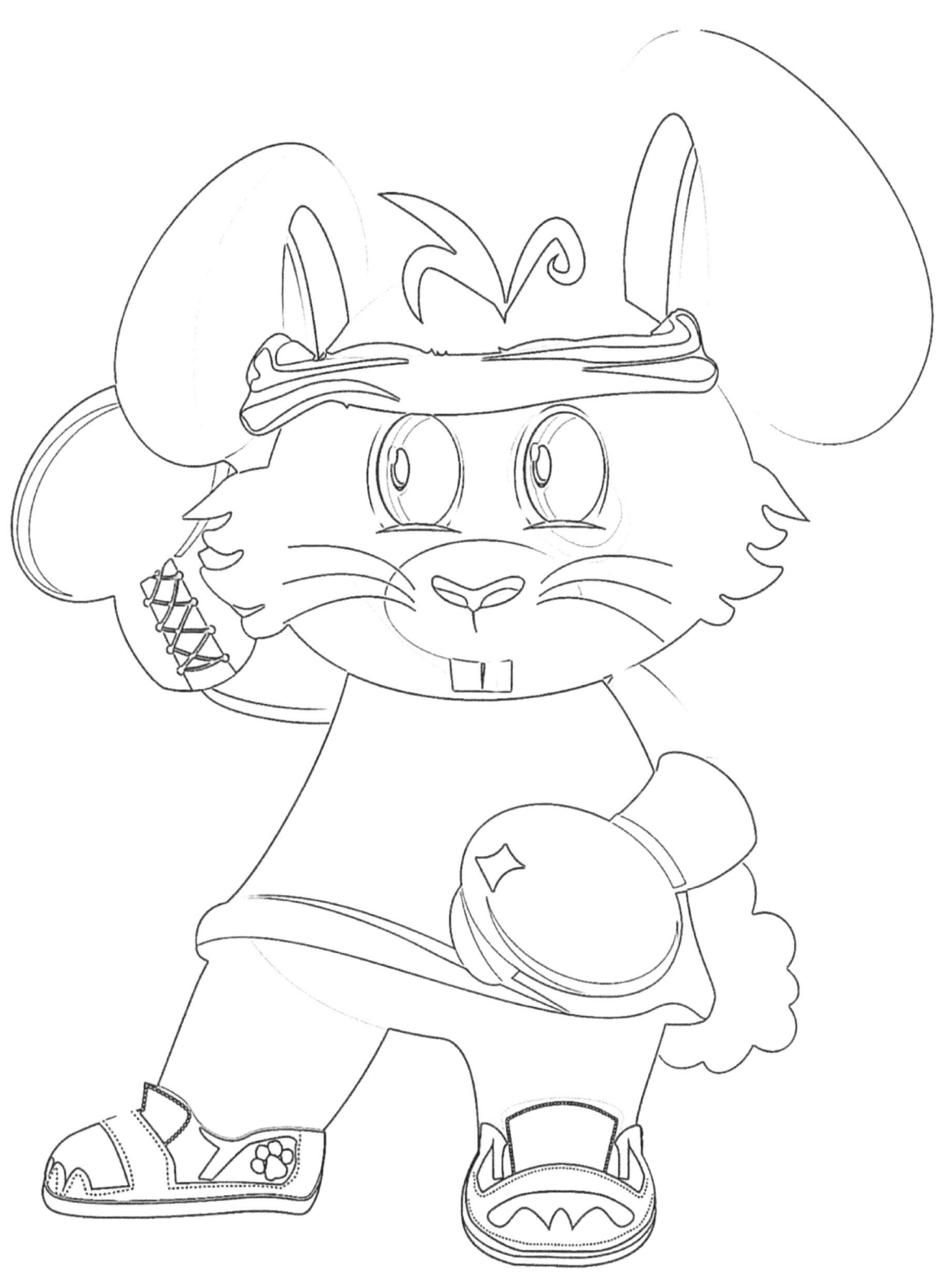

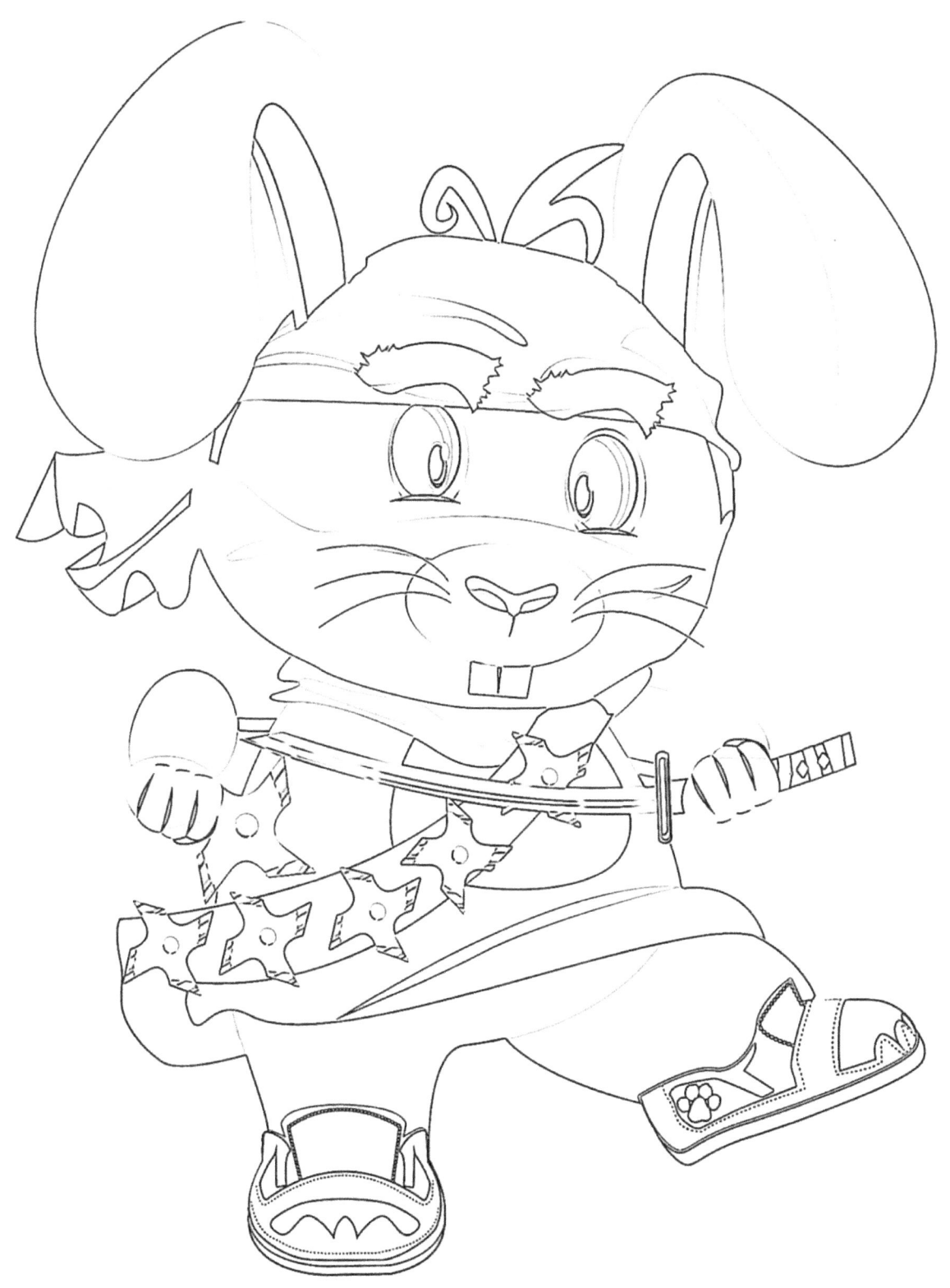

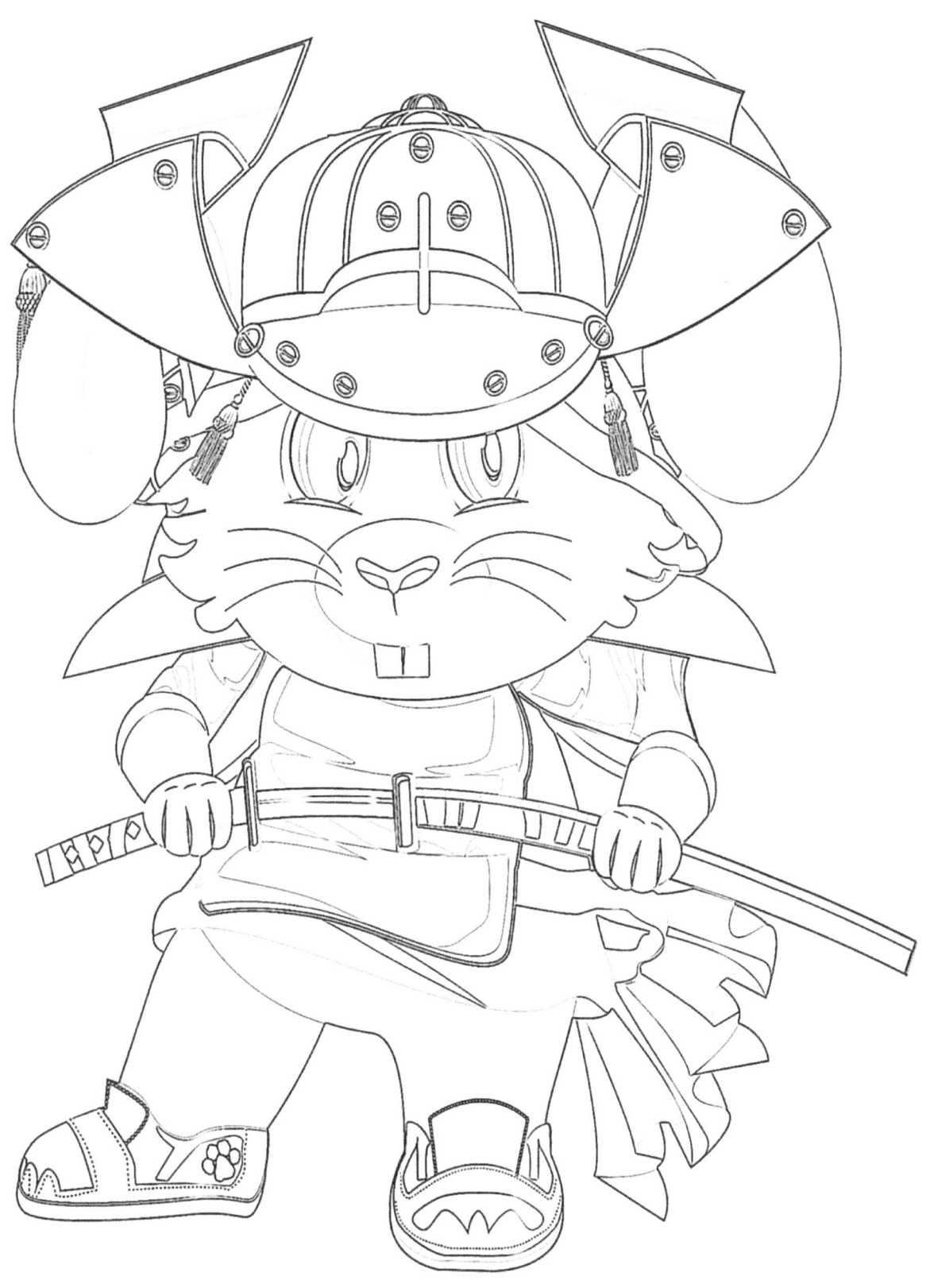

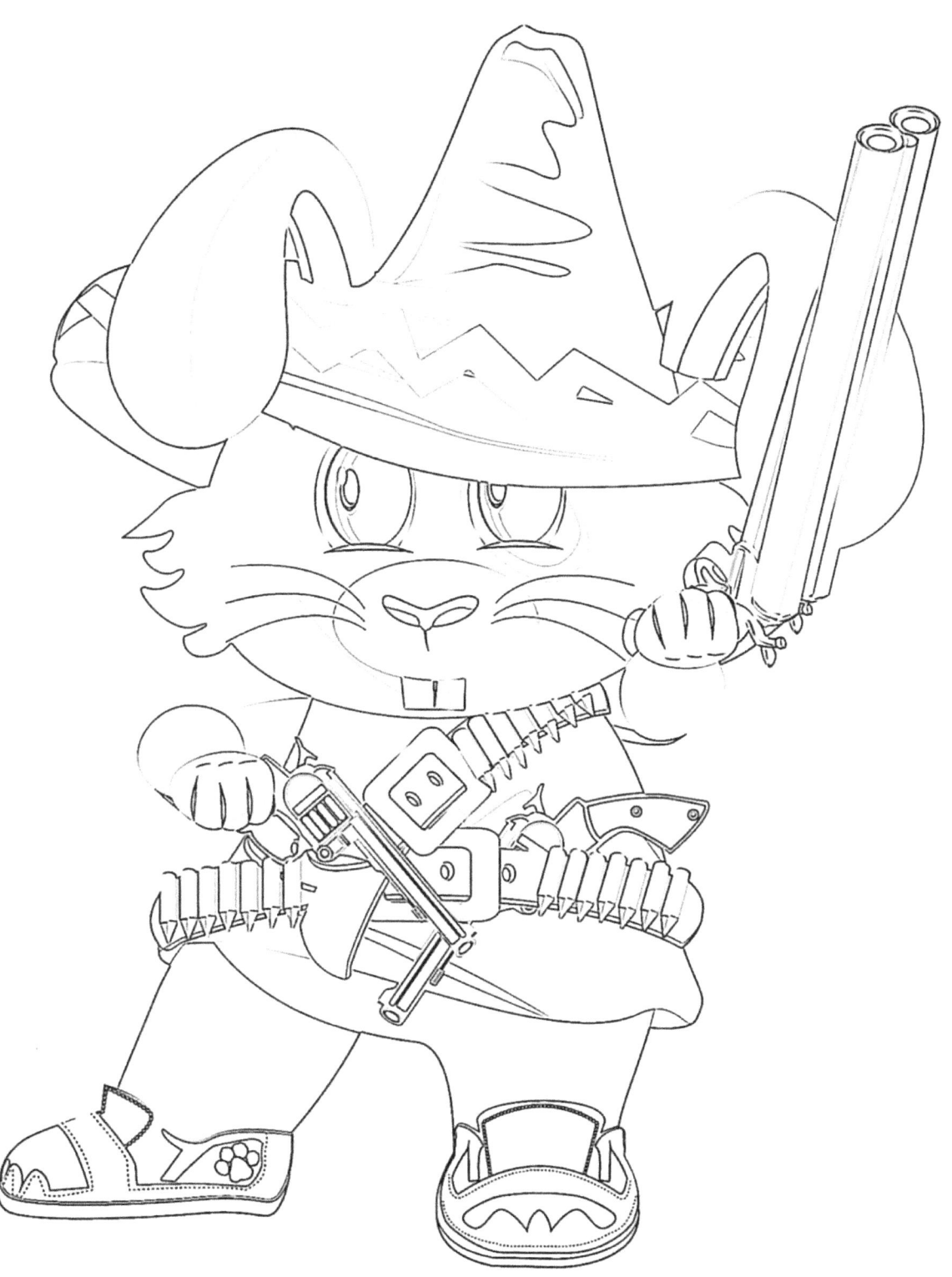

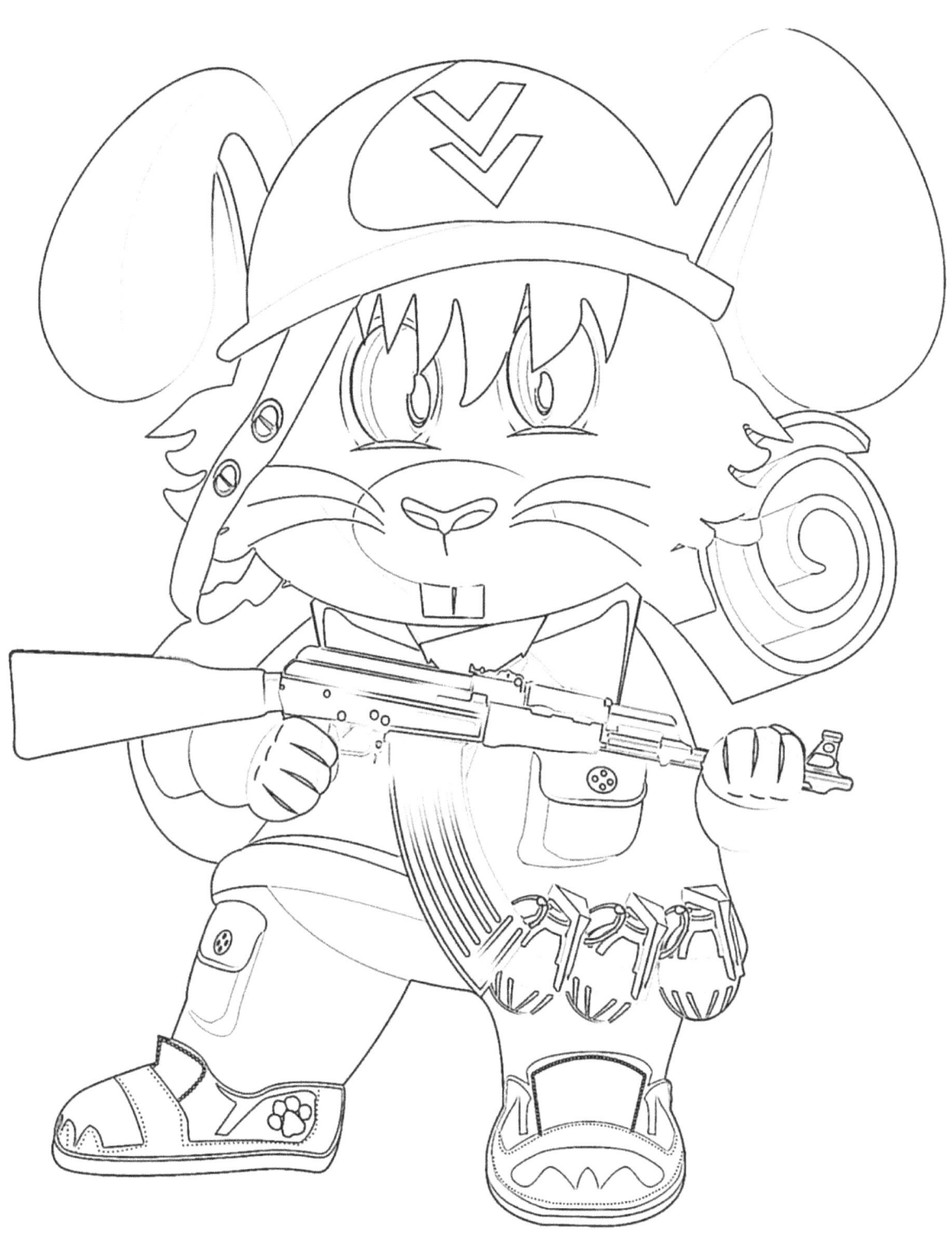

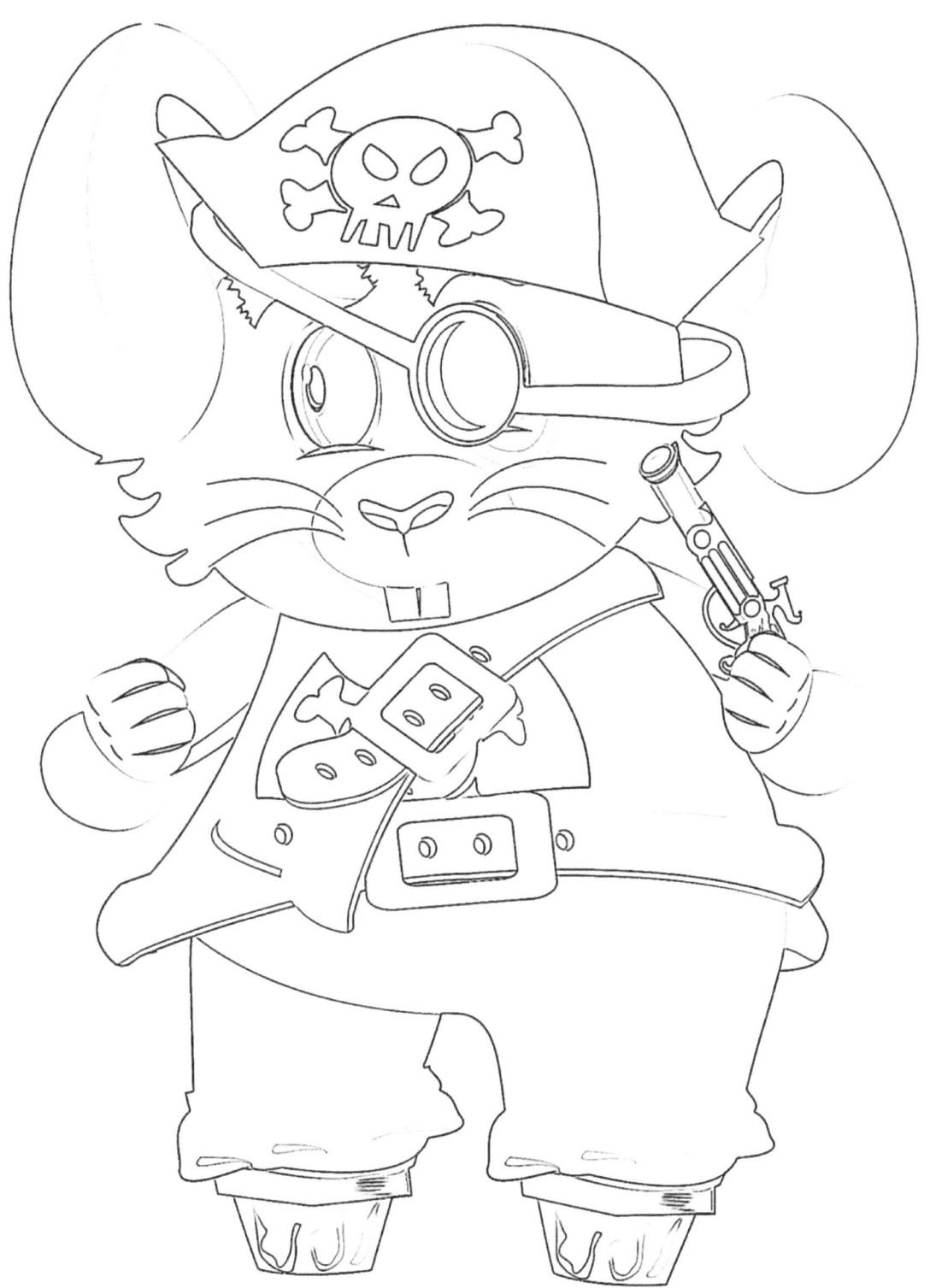

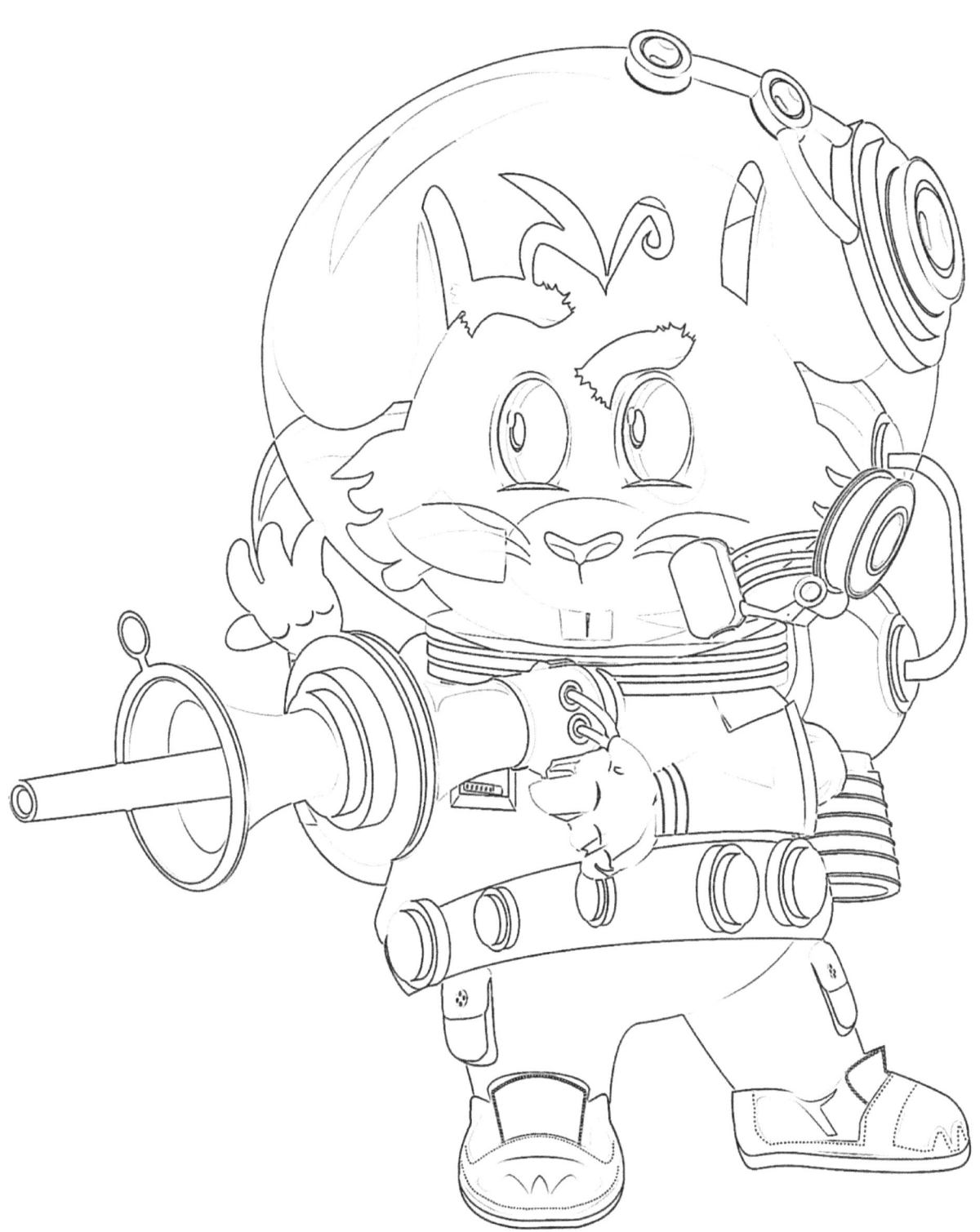

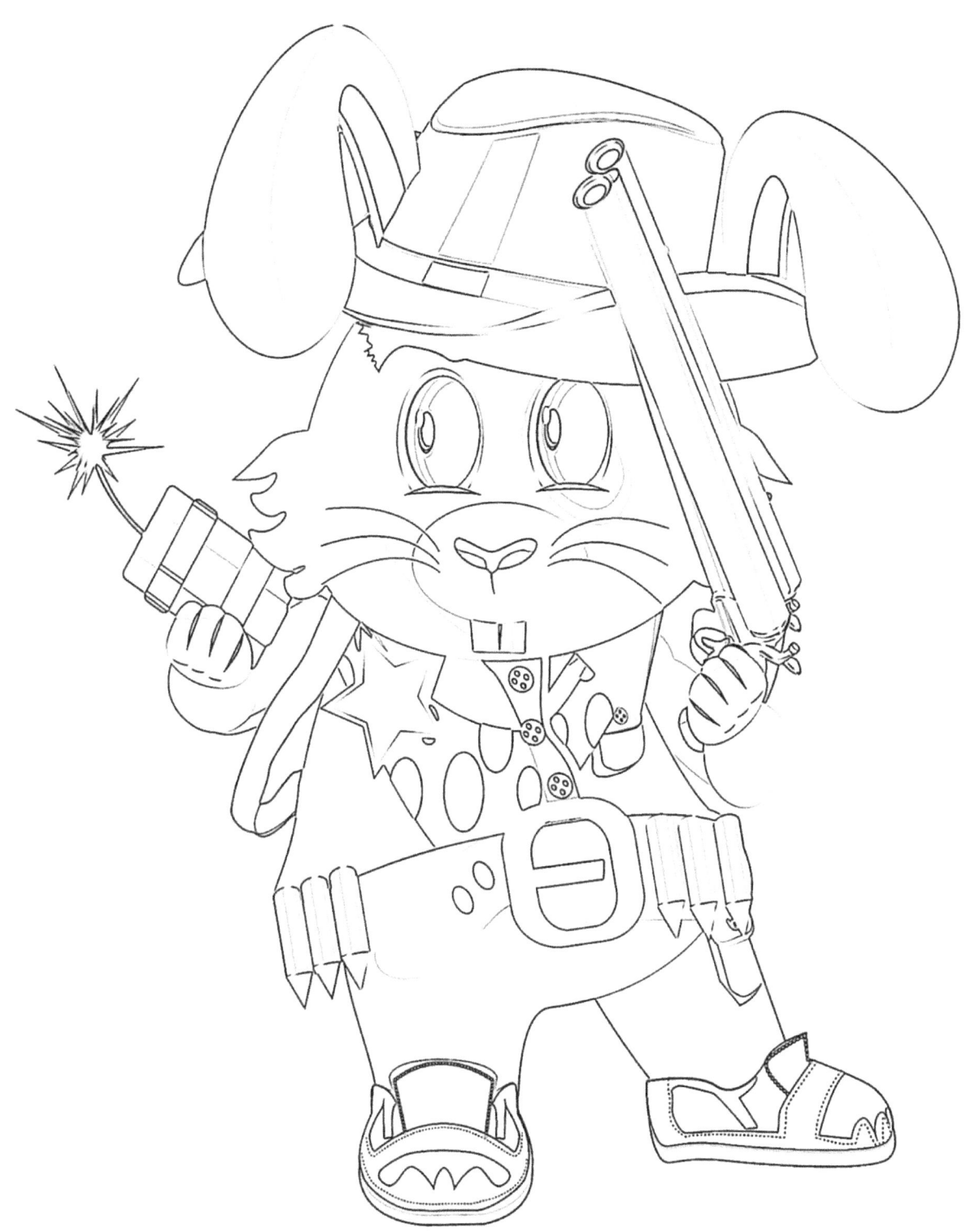

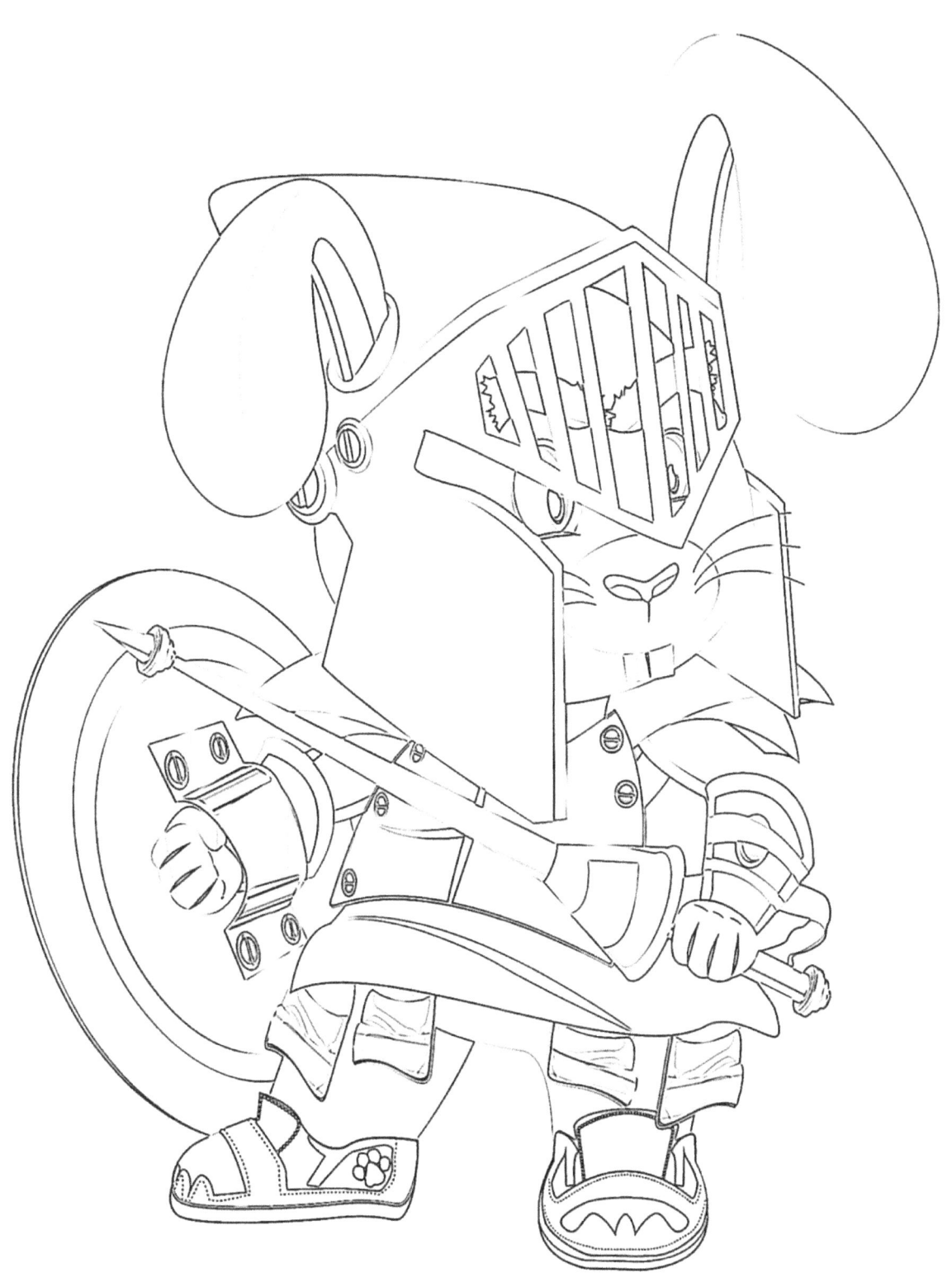

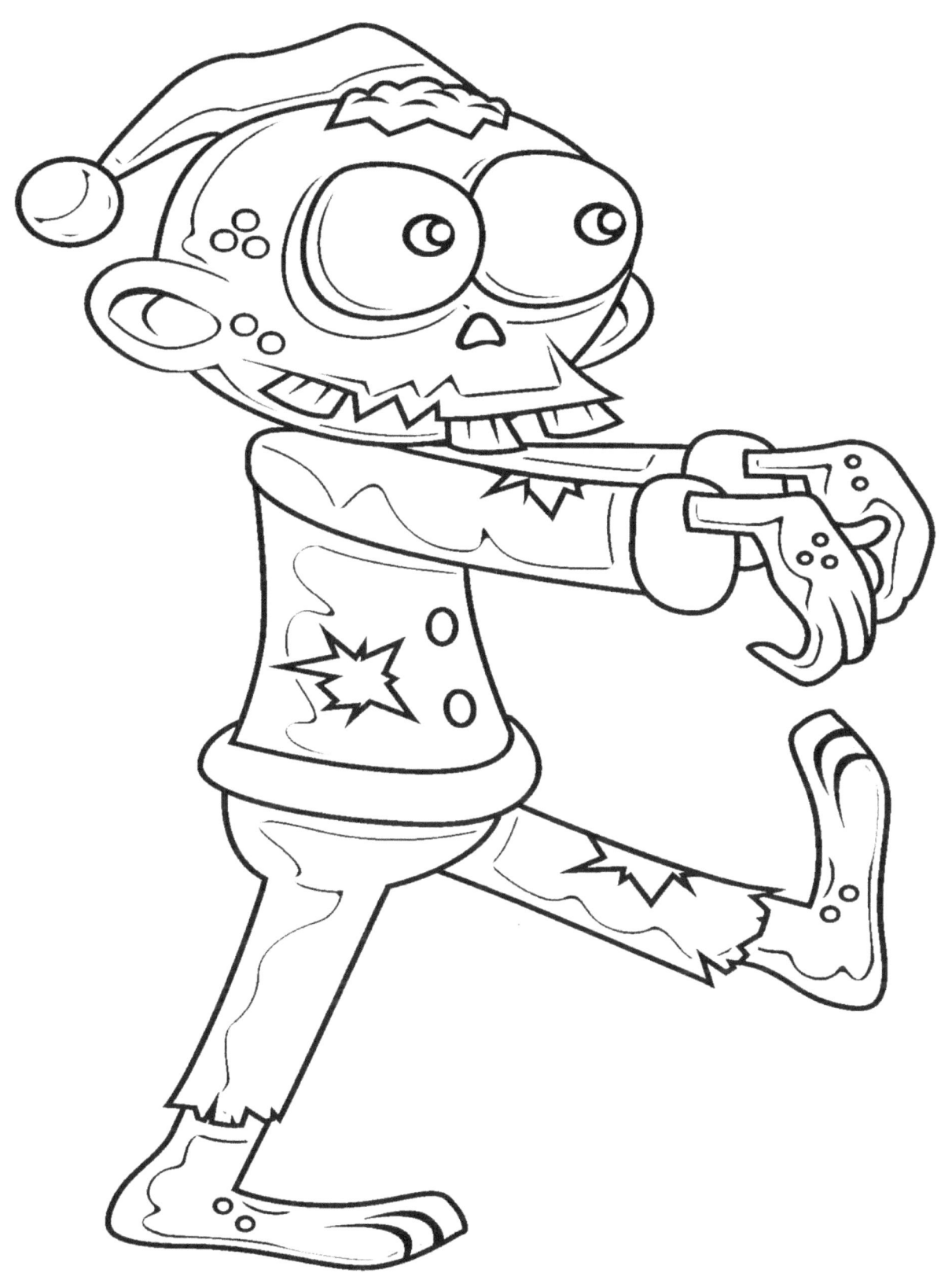

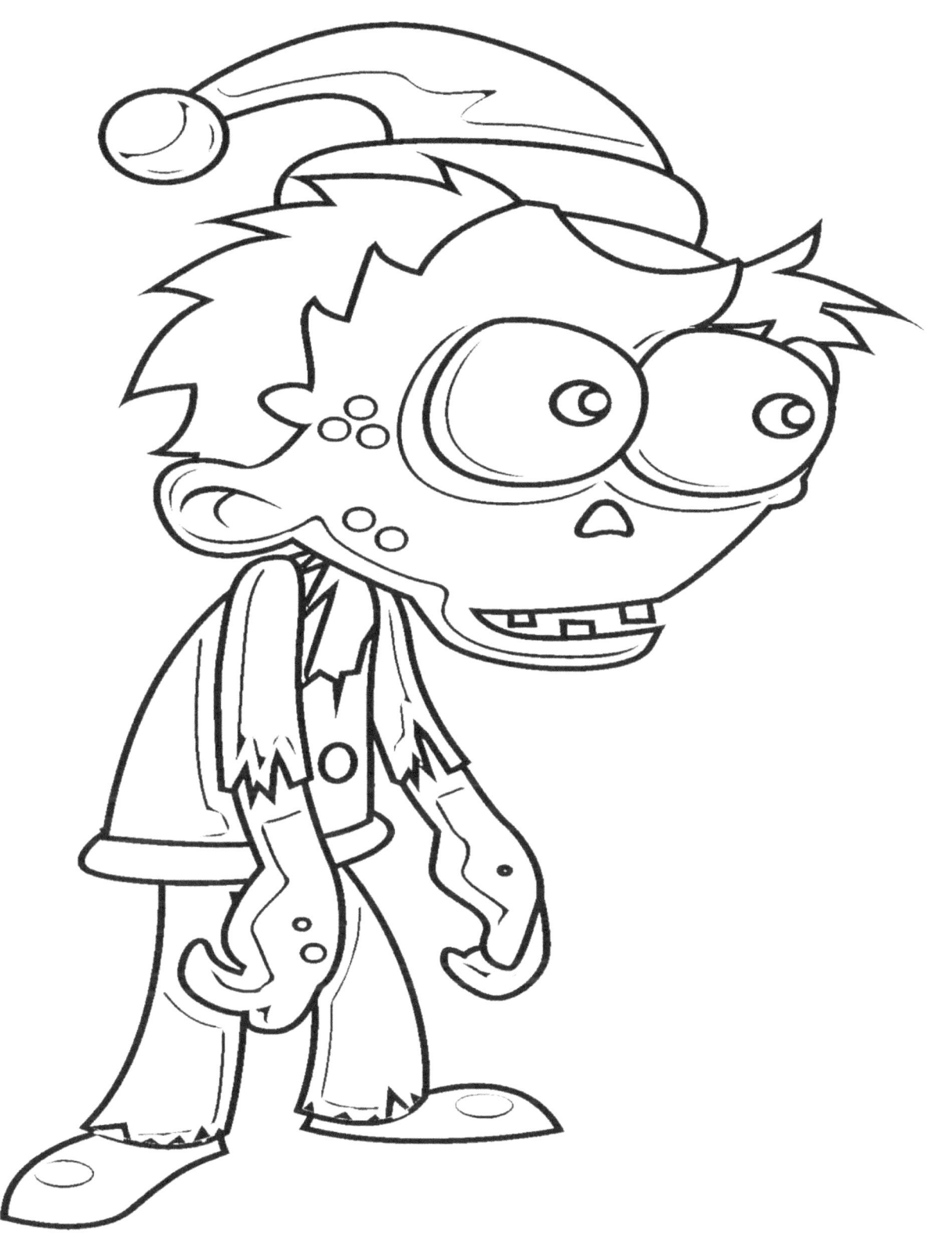

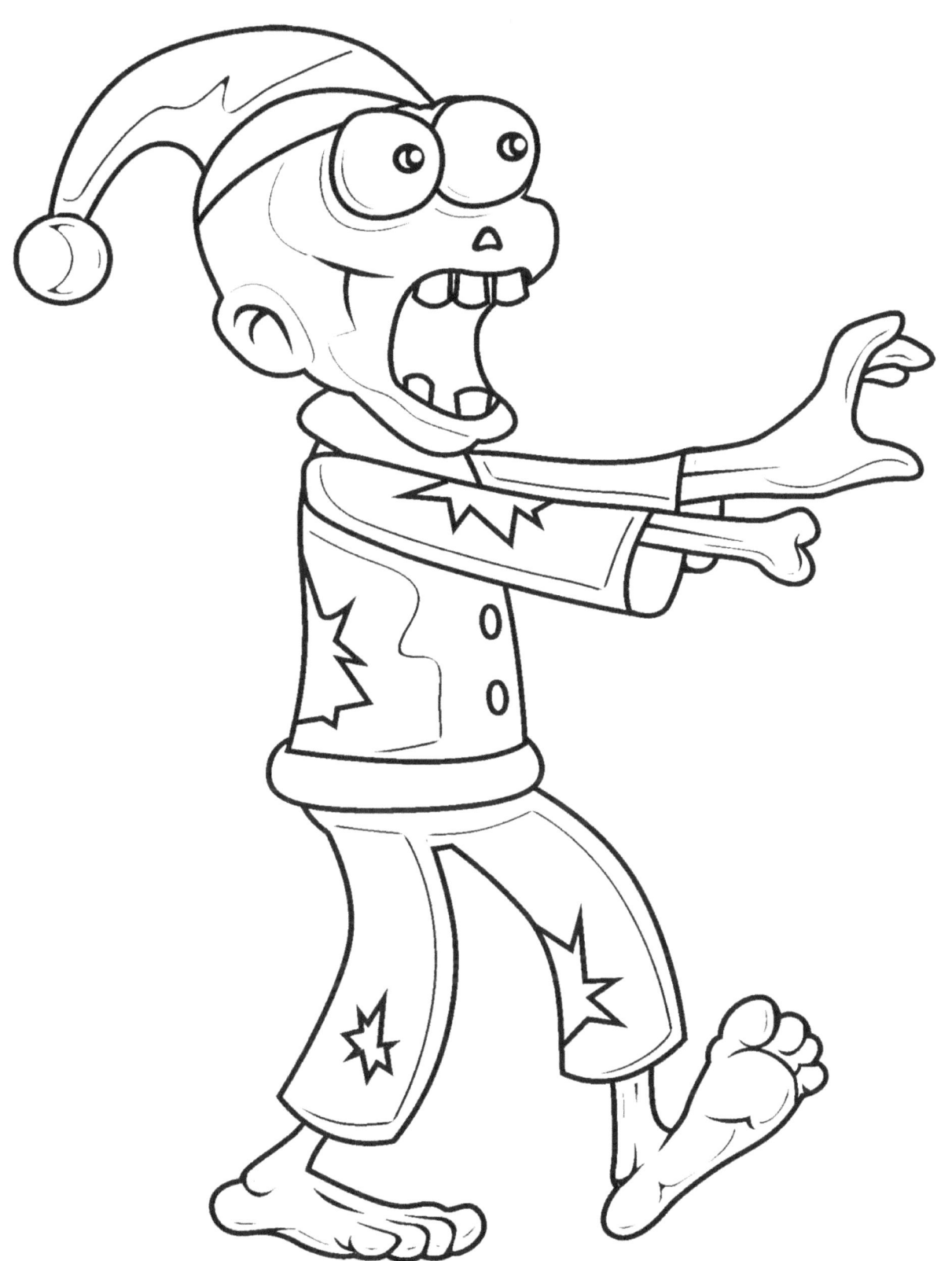

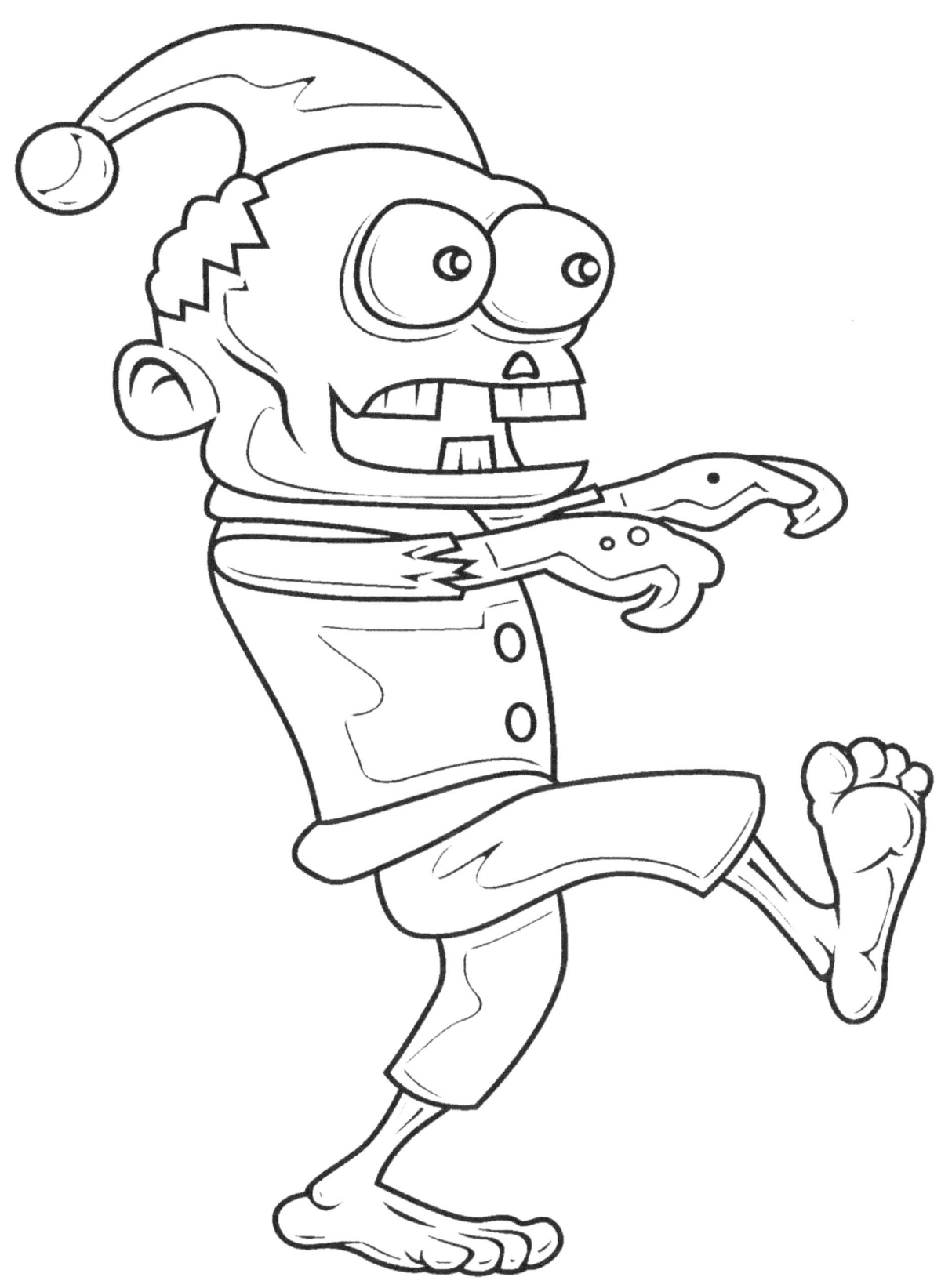

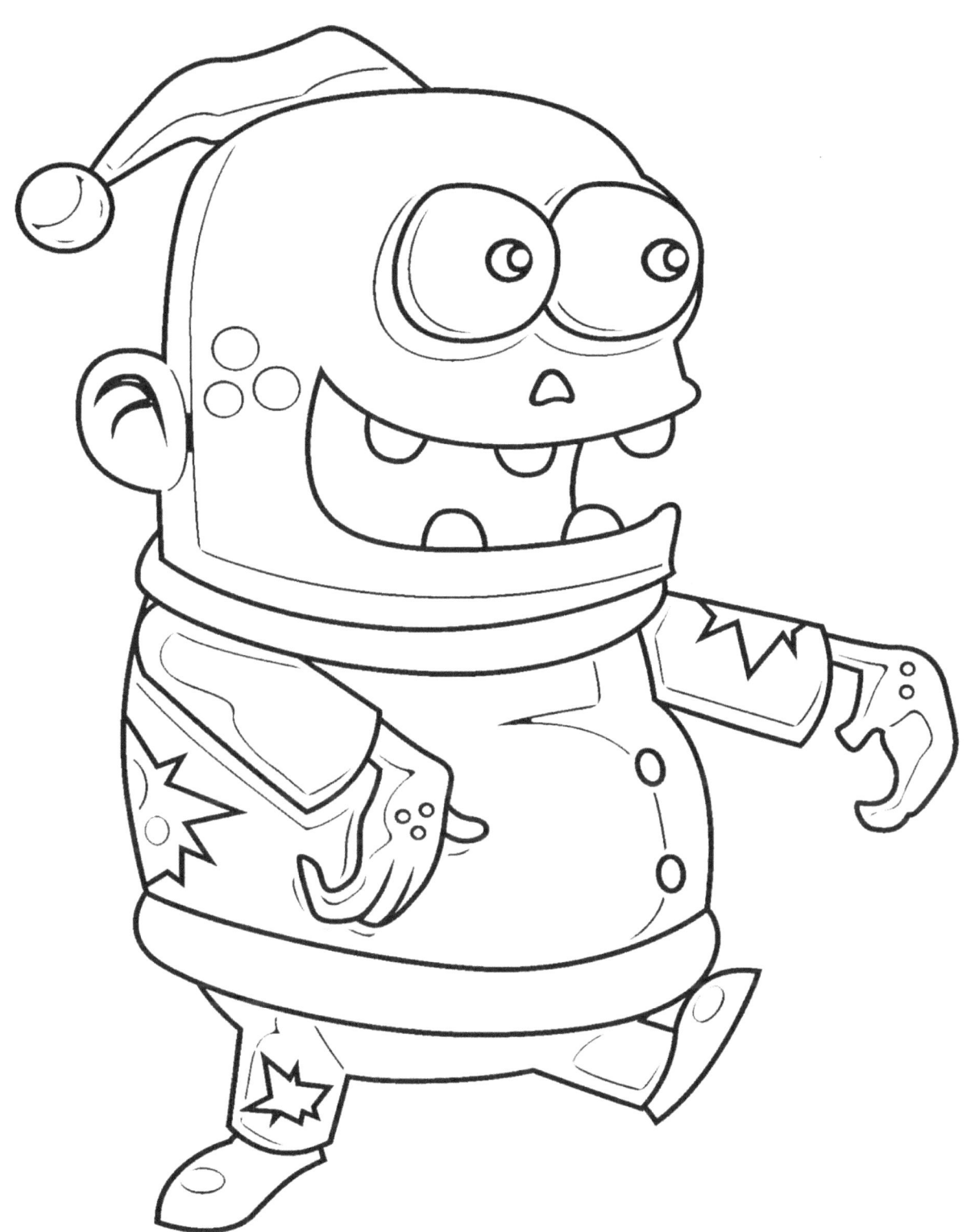

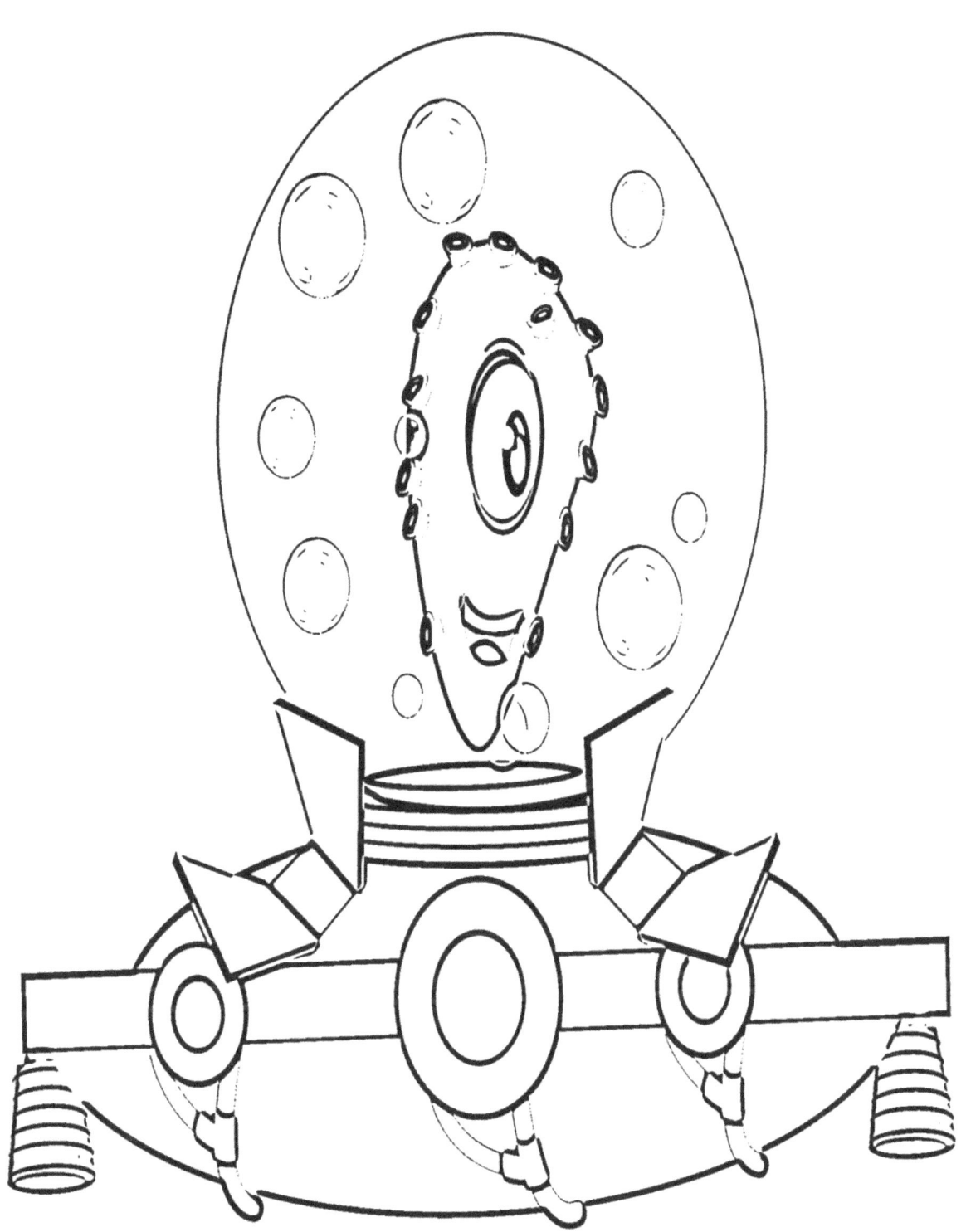

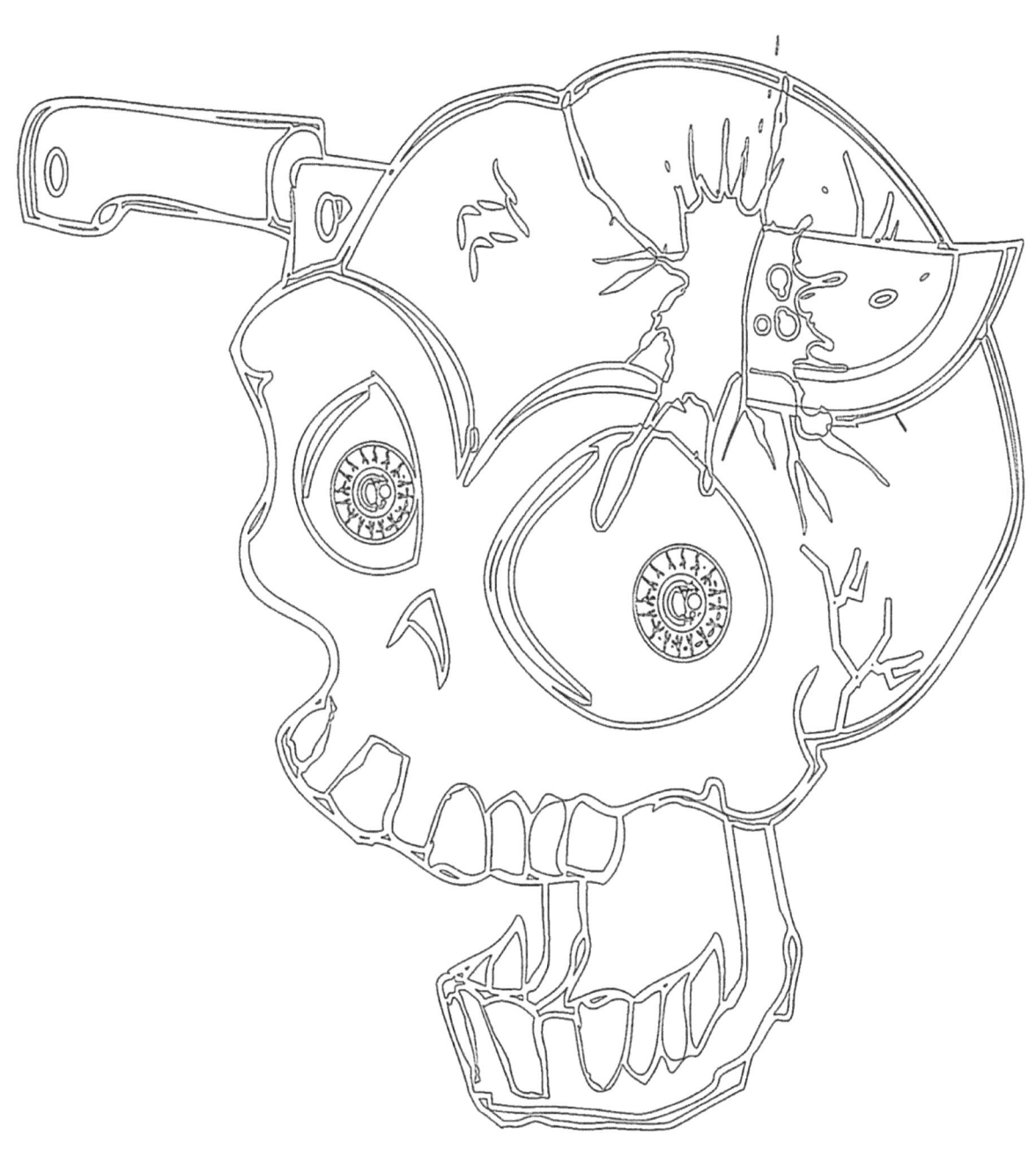

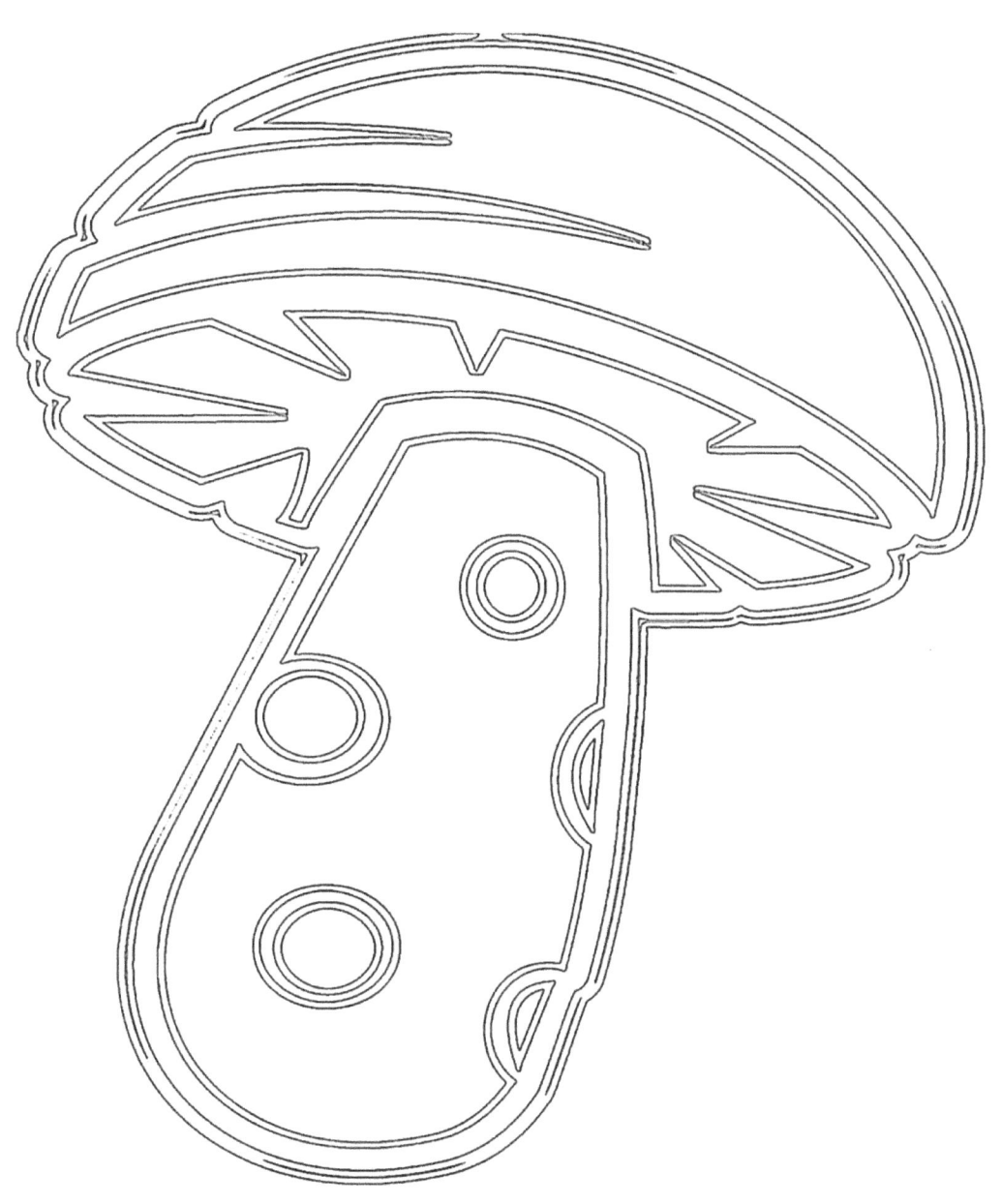

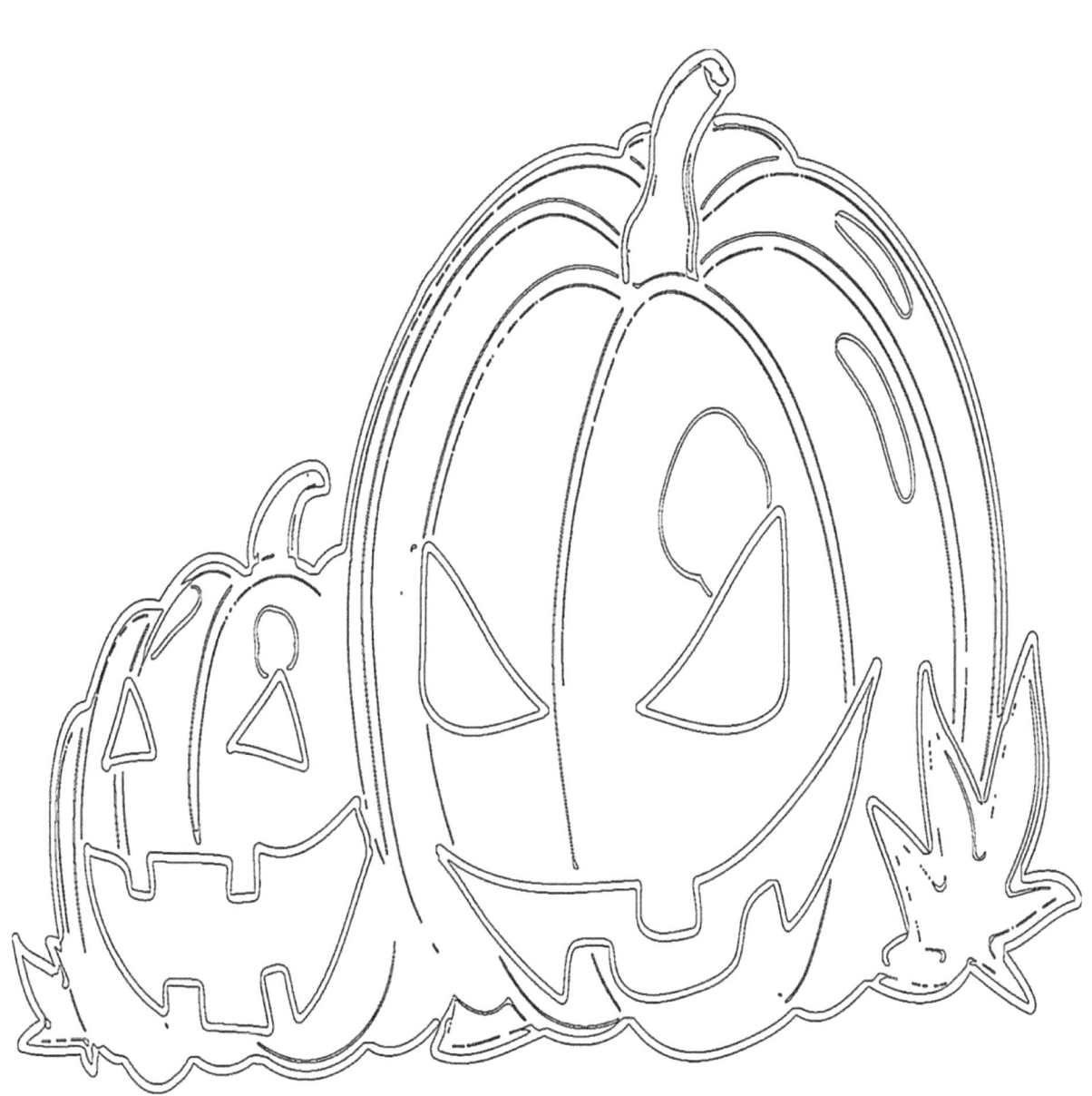

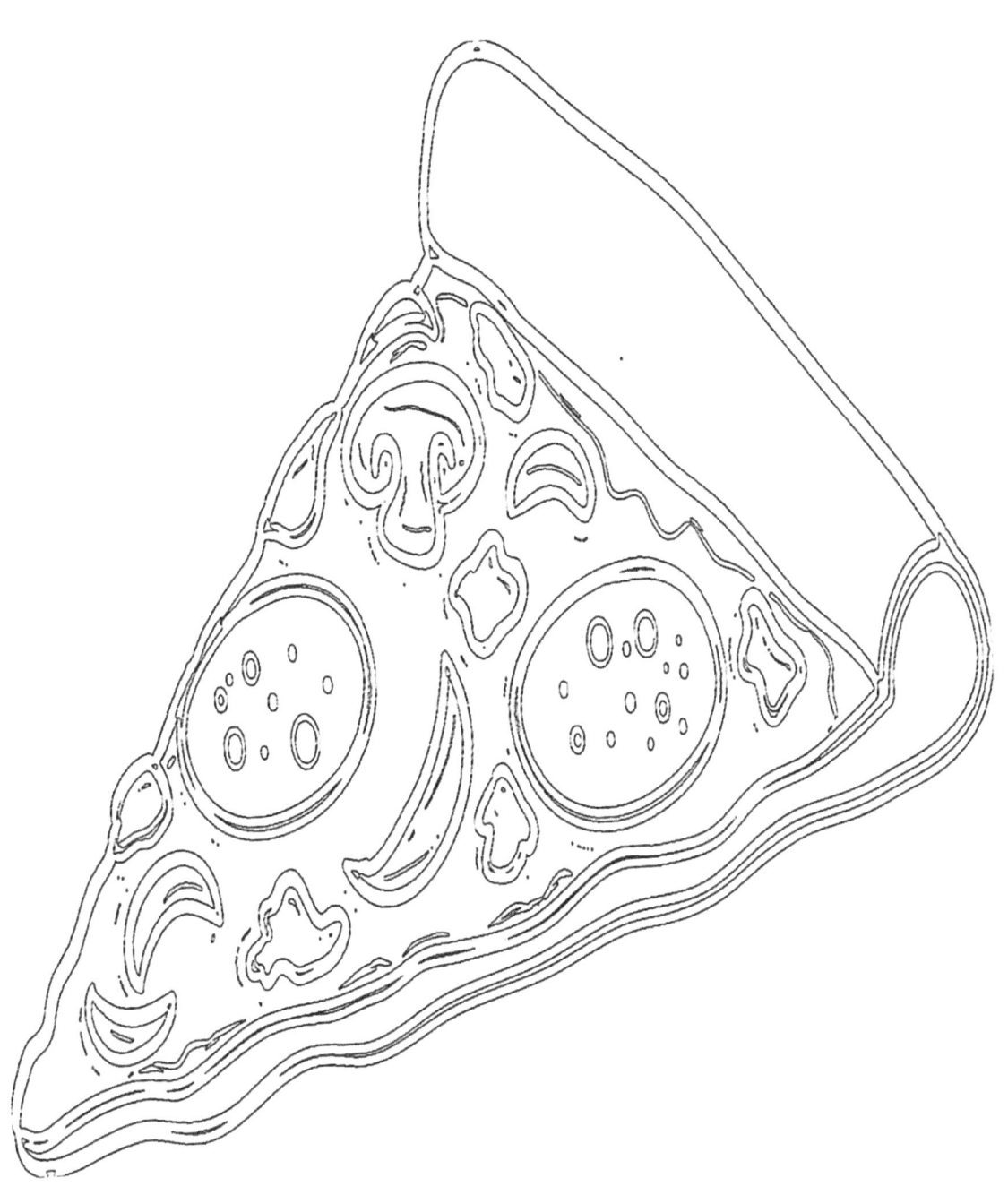

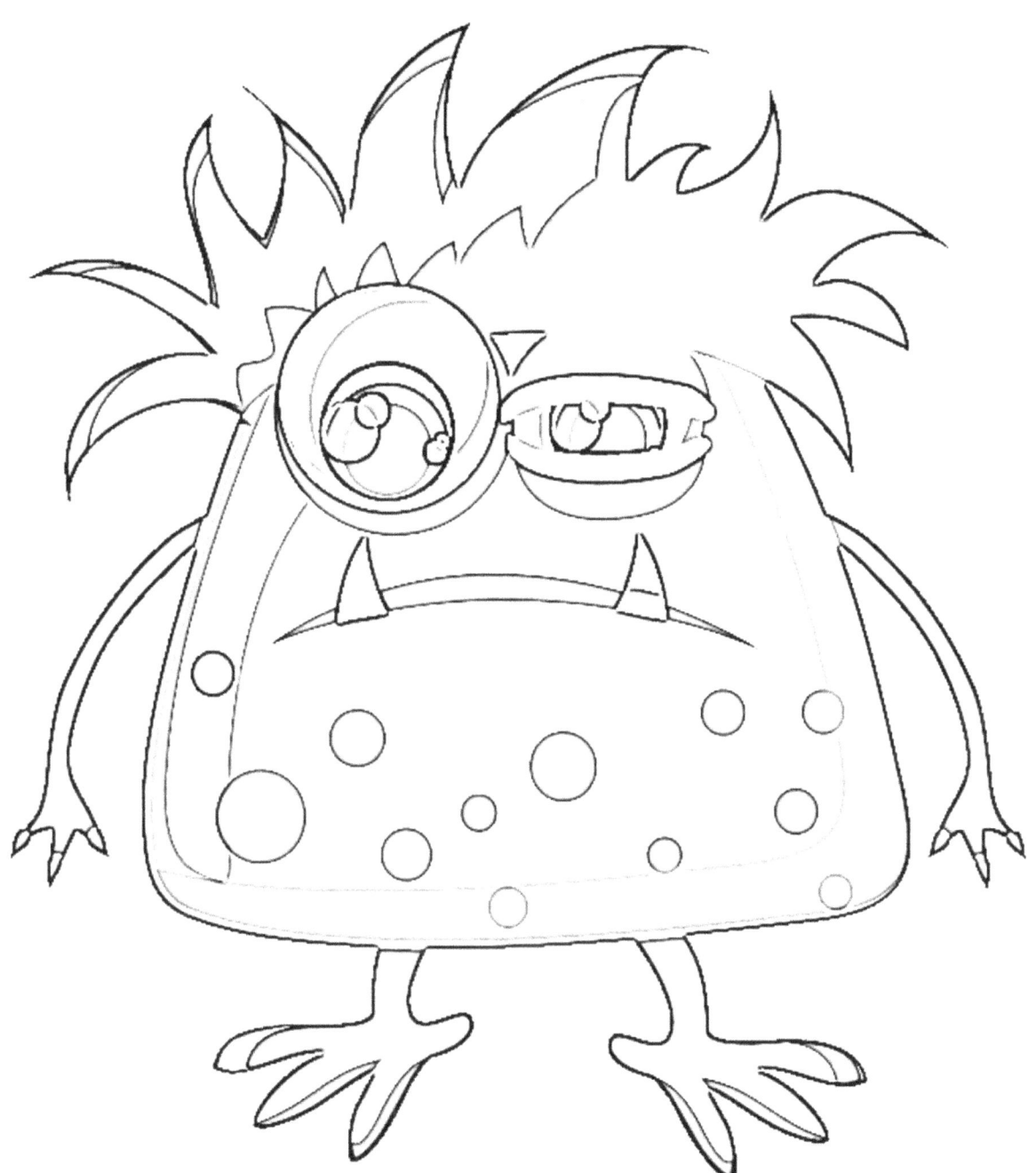

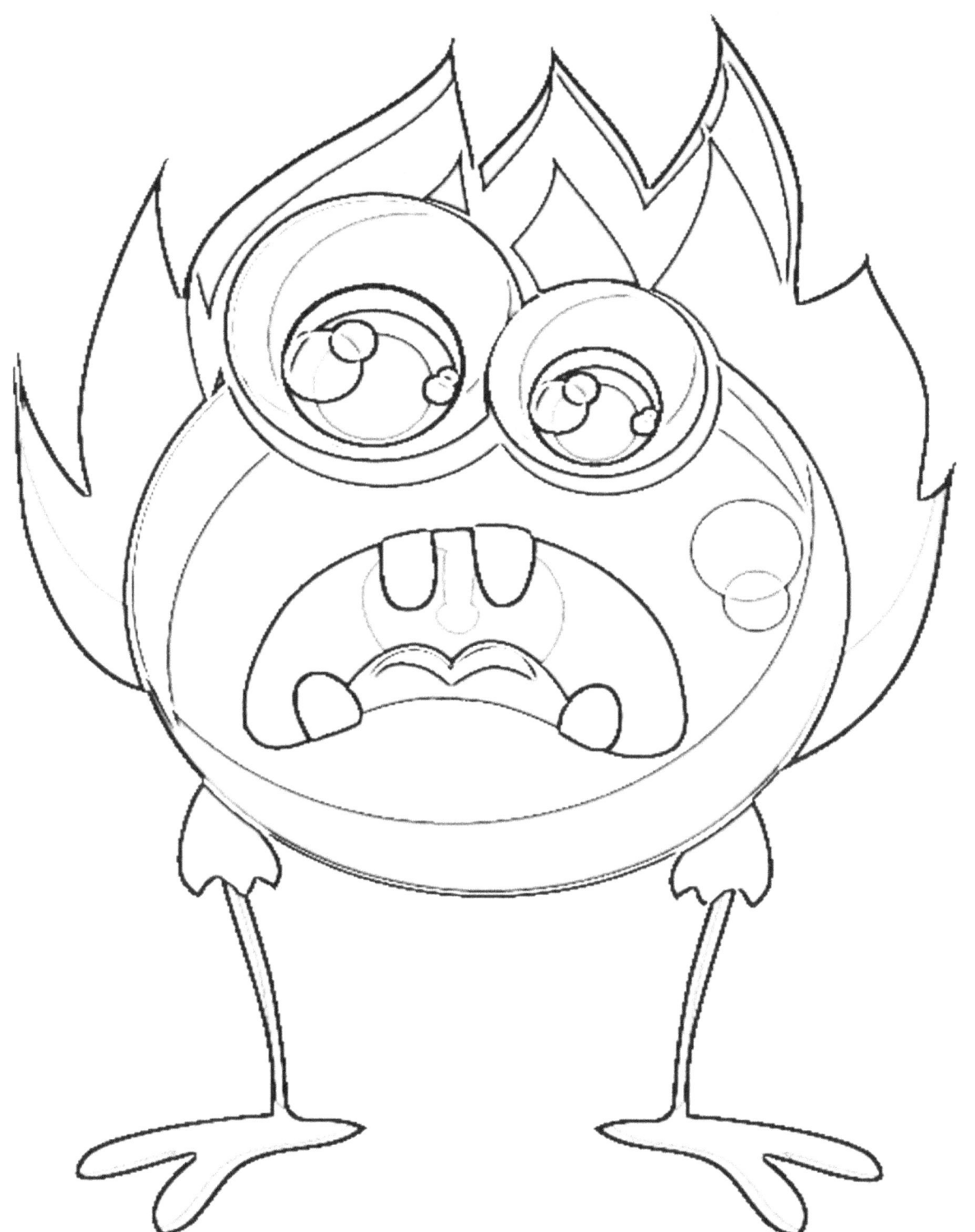

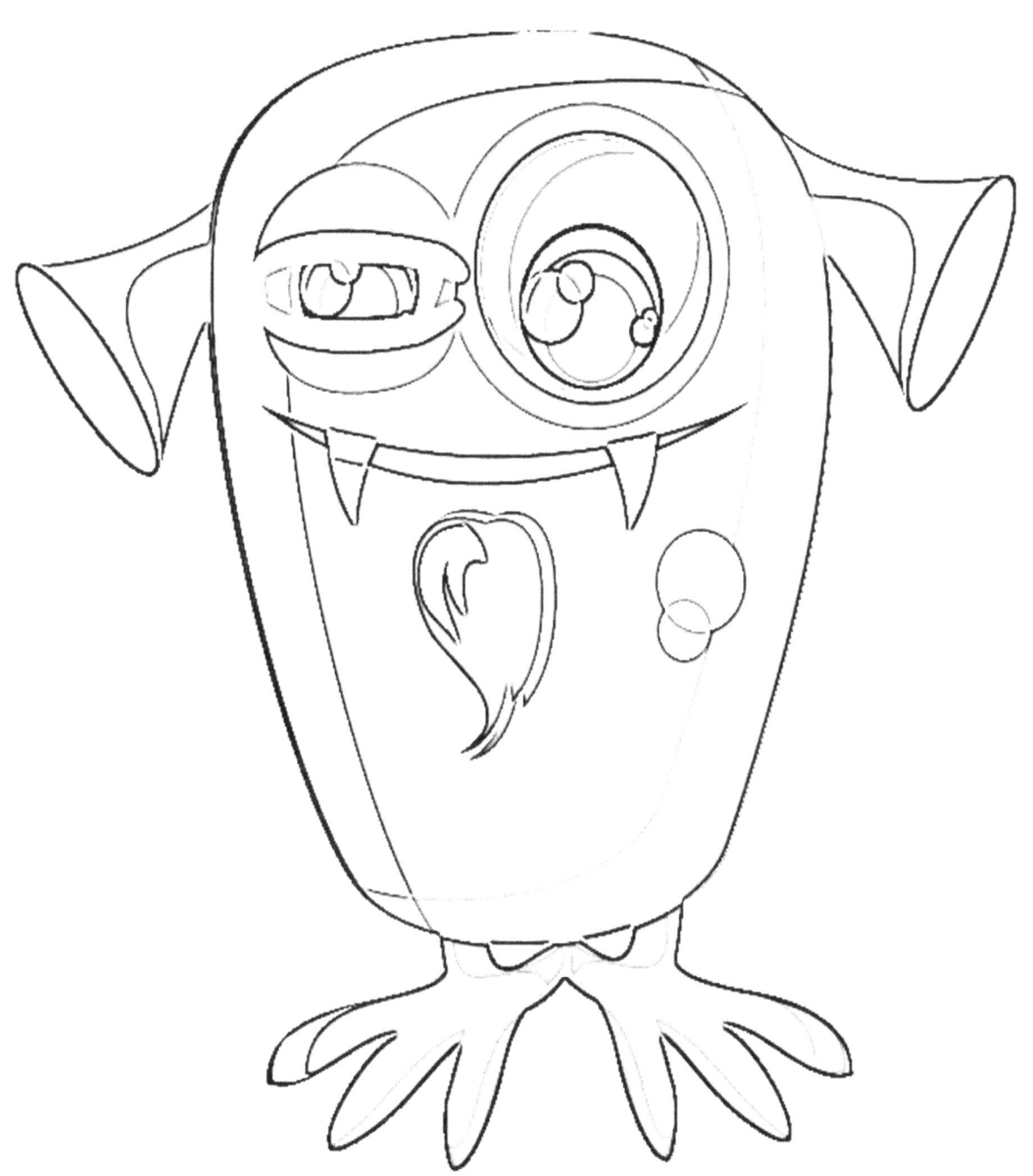

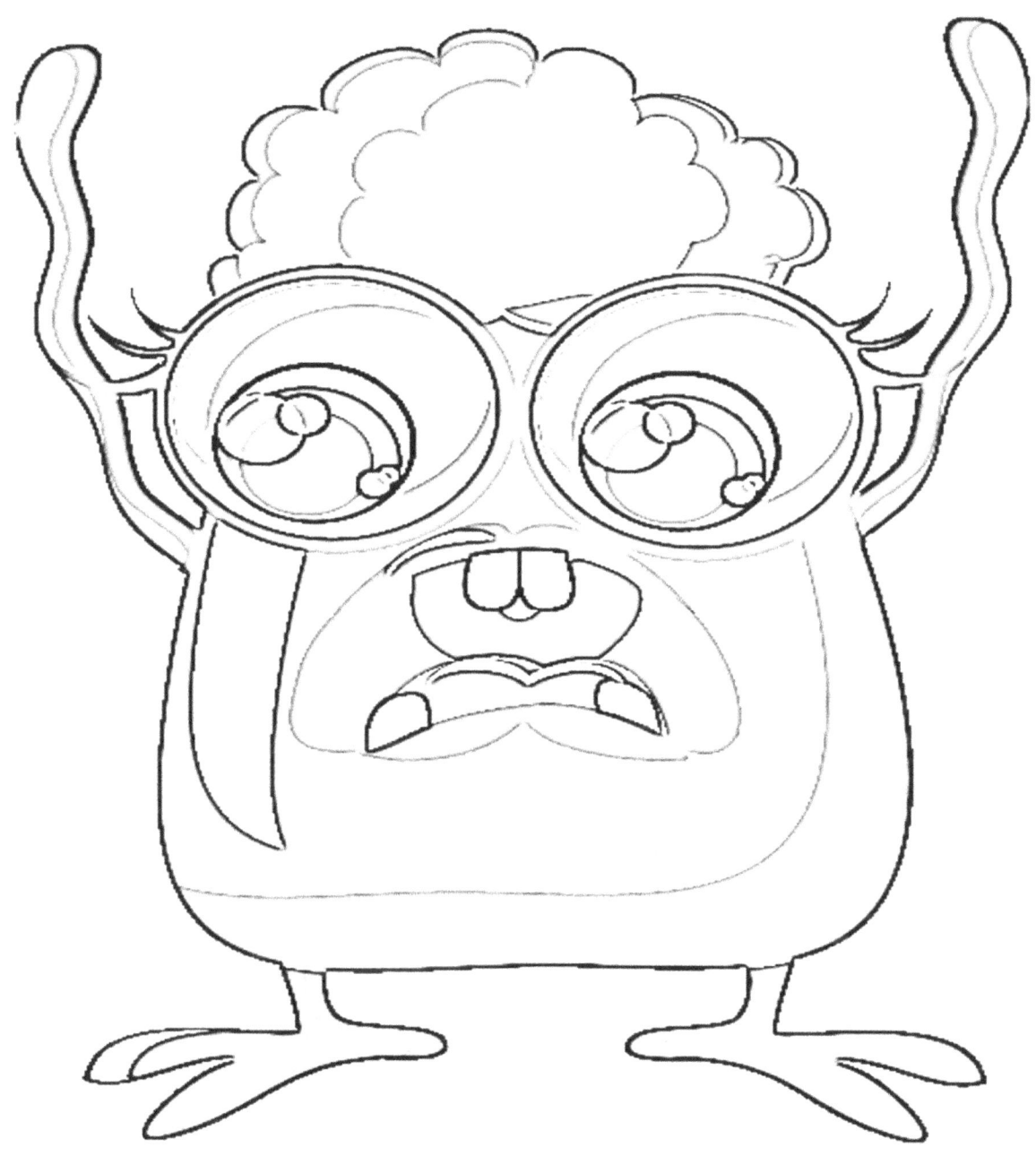

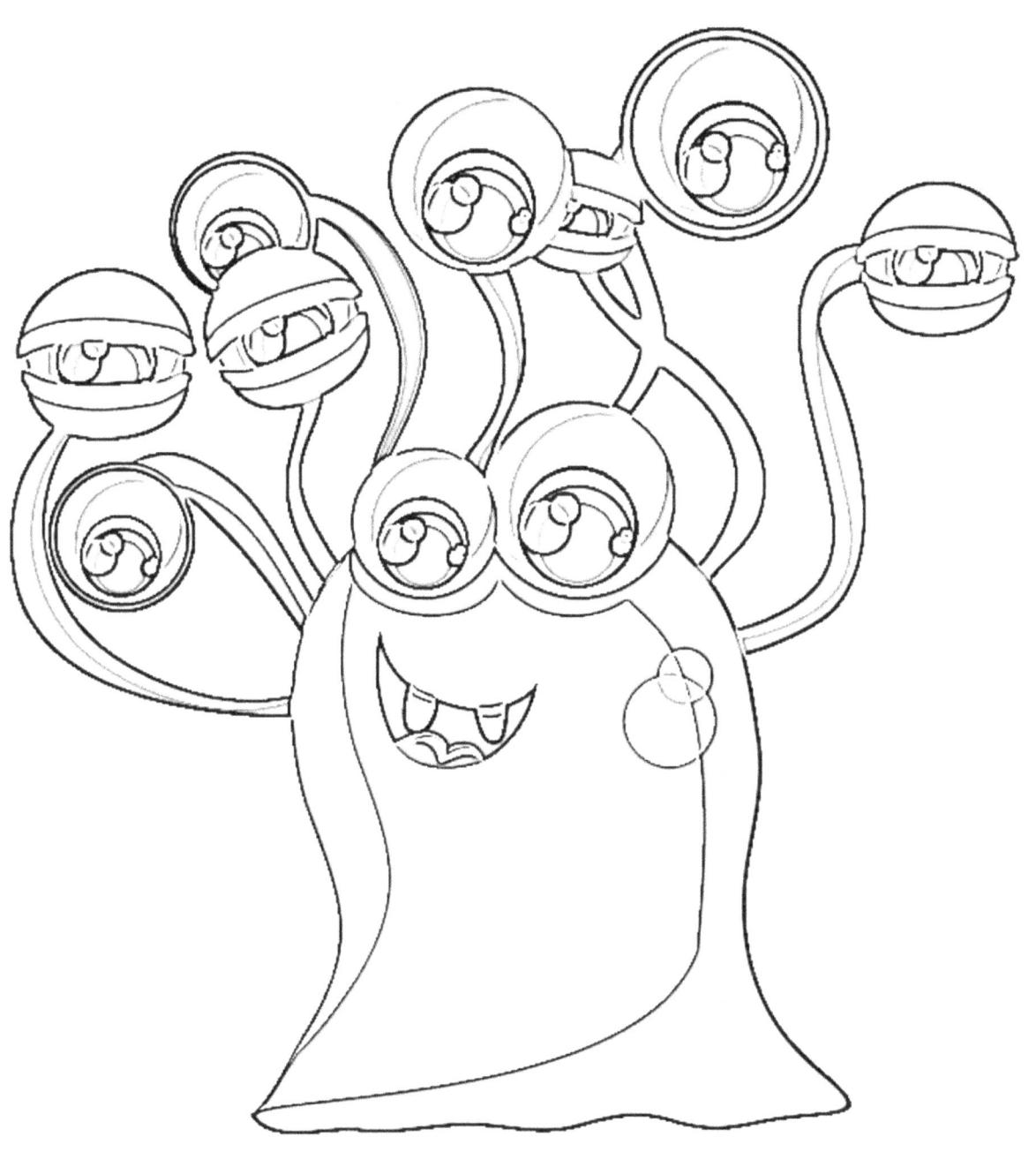

www.ingramcontent.com/pod-product-compliance
Lightning Source LLC
Chambersburg PA
CBHW081157180526
45170CB00006B/2112